ADVENTURES
WITH
ARCTIC WILDLIFE

Adventures with Arctic Wildlife

By

VIVIAN STAENDER

Photographs by
Gilbert Staender

Drawings by
Frank Staender

The CAXTON PRINTERS, Ltd.
Caldwell, Idaho
1970

Portions of this book were previously published as an article, "Birding with the Bears
in the Brooks Range" in *Mazama,* 1964,
and in *Summit,* a mountaineering magazine

574.9798
S 778a

Printed and bound in the United States of America by

The CAXTON PRINTERS, Ltd.

Caldwell, Idaho   83605

113221

To all the animals of the
Brooks Range who moved
over to allow us room to live
in their wildlife community

Acknowledgements

WE WISH TO ACKNOWLEDGE WITH GRATITUDE THE MANY people who made our journeys into the Arctic, and this book, possible. Special thanks go to the United States Fish and Wildlife Service for their interest and cooperation, to the Mazamas and two anonymous donors for material assistance. To Gil's parents, Frank and Ann, who looked after our home in Lake Oswego during our absence; to Bernice Sitton, R.N., for planning our first-aid kit.

We are grateful to Helen Smith, Richard Barden and Walt Morey for encouragement and suggestions when working with the manuscript; and to Loren, Kay, and Jay Shisler for the many hours' use of their darkroom.

We are honored to have an introduction by Margaret Murie.

GIL AND VIV STAENDER

Contents

Chapter   *Page*

Illustrations

10 ILLUSTRATIONS

Introduction

SOME OF US COMPLAIN ABOUT THE WORLD; SOME OF US DO something about it. Vivian and Gil Staender are doers, and there will be a chance of a better life for birds and beasts and the rest of us because these two young people did something.

In all the still-wild country left to us today lies the basic health of Man. He is proliferating and destroying and eating into and contaminating this treasury of his salvation; and at the same time he is trying to escape from his inventions to find himself, and here is the great anachronism. If more and more of us flee to the Wilderness for peace who then is to save the essence of Wilderness which is its untouched-by-man quality? Here is one of our present-day dilemmas.

The Staenders first planned to go to the Brooks Range simply to climb and hike and explore and enjoy. But because they had watched things happening to the birds in their Oregon garden, they found themselves involved with the United States Fish and Wildlife Service and collecting samples of young birds and eggs and other forms of life up there, and what the Fish and Wildlife scientists learned from these samples about pesticides and fallout must make us all shudder, and pray for a change in world politics!

The second thing that happened to Gil and Vivian

was total immersion in the "spirit of place." They fell in love with that wild yet gentle, rugged yet kindly, country, as every one of us who has been up there has done —and this love and happiness carry us along rejoicing with them all through Vivian's story. Having struggled and wept through a good many stretches of Arctic tundra-tussock myself and slogged through streams and willow brush, and watched grizzly bears with mingled joy and apprehension, I find the narrative fascinating, but I am sure every reader will be glad he opened this book, and when he closes it he will be richer in spirit and more eager to help preserve our last wild places.

A third point I want to stress; that is the great concern of Gil and Vivian to leave the country as they found it. I quote: "The time came to prepare for our trek back to Loon Lake. We folded our red tent and cleaned up our campsite in the spruces. Only a few smoky stones remained as evidence that we had invaded this unblemished wilderness."

If only this could be the creed of all who visit any clean, defenseless, wild place!

Speaking of a day spent on top of a mountain Vivian says: "The impact of our solitude was enormous. As though in a fantastically exquisite cathedral, we gazed over hauntingly beautiful wild peaks stretching endlessly in all directions. Only the wild creatures shared this tremendous untamed land with us, land that belonged to *them*. We were filled with a deep tranquility."

Gil and Vivian share the tranquility with us. They also bring to us the urge to do something about the future of our wild treasure. I pray their message will be heeded.

MARGARET E. MURIE
MOOSE, WYOMING

August, 1970

ADVENTURES
WITH
ARCTIC WILDLIFE

Chapter 1

Amid Tranquility, Recollection

> *The knapsack of custom falls off his back with the first step he makes into these precincts.**

WITH MOTOR ROARING AND WATER SPRAYING FROM THE floats, bush pilot Andy Anderson took off. Banking into a tight turn and heading south over the lake, the little plane flew around the shoulder of the mountain and disappeared.

Then time stood still. Deathlike, overpowering silence!

It was eight o'clock on a cloudy June evening when my husband and I stood with our survival equipment on the rocky shore of an austere alpine lake. For as far back as we could remember, we had been subjected to buzzing, droning, chugging, whining motors. For the past two and a half hours, we had been mesmerized by the din of deafening plane motors, pounding our eardrums. Now we were stunned by the sudden stillness. In bewilderment we listened to the awesome unfamiliar quiet!

"So this is the Arctic," I thought. Was I dreaming? How weird everything seemed. Scary.

We were on our own now. There was no turning back. For three months, we would be totally out of contact

---

*Chapter quotations throughout are from the writings of Ralph Waldo Emerson.

with civilization. We looked around at the strangeness
and I wondered if we'd opened our mouths once too often. Maybe I wasn't as brave as I thought I was. Barren
mountains glowered down on us. High above on the
west, dark foreboding crags. Beneath sheer cliffs, large
loose rocks tumbled down to the water line. East slopes
were clothed with patches of snow and dead-looking
grayish-brown vegetation. The narrow valley opened
up to the south, where row after row of wild snowy peaks
seemed to go on into eternity.

I looked at Gil to see if he was as frightened as I was.

"I guess I have a yellow streak," he said into the un-
earthly quiet. "I'm scared." He was looking all around.
"But we'll be all right—I think."

"Yeah," I muttered as I stepped closer to him. He
could take care of us—I hoped.

The two-mile-long Loon Lake, half covered with ice,
was pinched together in the middle, like an hourglass.
It looked so *sterile*. The water level was low. Cheerless
bare gray rocks framed the shore. Like on the surface
of the moon, no life-supporting vegetation—not even moss
—grew on the stones.

Ominous shadows accentuated the draws and gullies.
A brisk, raw north wind sprang up to send shivers up my
spine.

"What a desolate place," Gil muttered.

"Brrr!" I shuddered. "Where are the spruces?"

According to the way we had read our topographic
map, Loon Lake, far north of the Arctic Circle, should
have the last spruces of the northern tree limit. The only
"trees" we could see were a few tall lanky shrubs of alders
and willows, just leafing out.

We knew we were in grizzly country. With no trees,

LOOKING DOWN ON AN ARCTIC RIVER, FLYING
IN TO LOON LAKE
Notice the frozen lakes, and the "mosaic," caused by freezing and thawing

there was no safe place to cache our food. No safe place
to go in case of attack. We had the .375 magnum rifle
as our sole means of protection. Gil had a shotgun and
.22 pistol for bird specimens.

With binoculars, we carefully searched the forbidding slopes. Grizzlies would be the same dun color as
their stark habitat. Gill had the rifle loaded. We saw no
movement.

❋   ❋   ❋

Our story really begins a year earlier at our suburban
home at Lake Oswego, Oregon.

Gil and I had read Rachel Carson's *Silent Spring*. We
read how chlorinated hydrocarbons affect birds, how one
of the first symptoms of pesticide poisioning is that the
young hatch but soon die. More contamination causes

sterility. Even more contamination causes loss of the mating urge, and finally death.

"But things aren't really that bad," we told each other. "We haven't noticed any dead birds lying around. There are so many robins wintering here, and other birds. Our Western Bluebirds are doing just fine. Haven't they had two or three successful broods each summer for the past five years?"

All Miss Carson's dire warnings seemed far away—not affecting us.

That was before the spring of 1963.

We didn't know anything was wrong that spring when the bluebirds returned from the south. Spring had sprung. Eternal spring, with bright new hope. Our tame bluebird, "Maurice" (named for Maurice Maeterlinck), was back with his mate to begin nesting again. From our bedroom window, we watched the busy pair carry fresh nesting material—fine grasses, bits of cotton and a few feathers—into the birdhouse. Their flashing blue wings brightened the spring days.

Gil and I recalled the previous year when we had watched a three-weeks-old fledgling bluebird, lone survivor from the first brood, fly to the perch of the birdbox. Baby bird heads reached out of the opening with wide open yellow-edged mouths. The speckled juvenal (we called him "Morris Minor"), still looking like a baby bird himself, promptly poked a beakful of insects far down into the throat of one of his hungry siblings. Then the "teen-age" older brother pecked playfully at the nestlings before flying off to gather more food.

We know of no other species of bird with such close family ties. It is not unusual for mated pairs of some bird species to have a strong "pair-bond," or even to mate for life, and for the family to stay together for the season. But juvenal bluebirds actually help with the rearing of succeeding broods of siblings of the same season.

A few years before, Gil and I had considered bird watchers a strange lot, succumbing to the popular stereotype of bird watchers—queer little old ladies in tennis shoes. At one time, ornithologists were considered lower on the totem pole than other biologists. Since then, scientists have found that birds can show intelligent behavior, nearly equal to that of dogs. Ornithology has thus become respectable.

Now it was different with us too. After observing the family activities of *Sialia mexicana,* we were hooked. *Bluebirds actually had personalities!* By 1963 Gil and I were looking forward to another summer's observations of these fascinating creatures.

A week after the nest was built, Maurice and his mate watched without alarm while we opened their nestbox and counted four blue eggs. But after incubation, only one egg hatched, and that young bird lived only two days. The other eggs were sterile. Never before had our bluebirds had sterile eggs.

Undaunted, these blue members of the thrush family moved to another birdbox, closer to our bedroom window, to begin all over again. Five eggs were deposited in the new nest.

Maurice flew down to pick up an insect. He fed it to his mate, as a token of his affection. She would soon begin incubation.

Glancing out of the window later that same day, I noticed that the female bluebird, on the birdhouse perch, was acting strangely. I called Gil. We watched as she struggled to enter the nest hole—in vain. She trembled.

She could no longer cling to the perch. Then she fluttered down and died in tremors on the ground.

Alone, the male guarded the five blue eggs. We waited three days, wondering if he would incubate them, as males sometimes do. But he only guarded.

We watched Maurice sitting disconsolately on the birdhouse, his mate dead.

"Isn't there something we could do for him?" I asked in agitation.

"We could put the eggs in the White-crowned Sparrow's nest," Gil suggested.

"That wouldn't be fair to the White-crowns. Besides, they would feed the young bluebirds seeds instead of insects."

"Couldn't we make an incubator?"

"Okay. Let's give it a try. We have nothing to lose."

We put three of the eggs in an incubator rigged up in a shoe box, with light bulb and thermometer. One egg was placed in the White-crown's nest and one egg was left for Maurice to guard. We hoped he would stay around to feed the young, once they hatched.

For a few days, we cared for the eggs in the incubator by sprinkling lightly and turning twice a day.

"Let's candle the eggs to see if they're any good."

We made a hole in a cardboard tube. A light was placed inside, and by holding the eggs before the lighted hole, we could see an embryo developing in the egg being incubated by the White-crown and another one in our makeshift incubator. Gil and I took heart.

But all our efforts were for naught. Both embryos died in their shells. Meanwhile the last bluebird, Maurice, had vanished.

We drove around our neighborhood watching the

HOUSE FINCH NEST (Carpodacus mexicanus)
containing four sterile eggs which had been
incubated two weeks.

Collected May, 1963 by Gilbert Staender
on fire thorn vine on N.E. corner of house.

OUT OF FIVE NESTS, THE FINCH EGGS WERE ONE
HUNDRED PERCENT STERILE

telephone wires for perching bluebirds, hoping to see
Maurice. What a shock to find that the species, a common sight in previous years, was becoming scarce. In
fact, we saw not a single bluebird in the Willamette Valley that summer.

Puzzled by what had happened to the bluebirds, Gil
and I determined to observe the nesting activities of
other birds on our one-third acre. What we found was
alarming.

Two pair of House Finches nested in the vines around
our house. We observed carefully when they built their
nests. Singing brightly all the while, the gallant males
were escorts on each trip for nesting material, each trip
to the birdbath—where it was always "ladies first." During incubation, they serenaded their wives and inspected
the eggs.

We candled the eggs after incubation. They were sterile.

Cheerfully, the finches began all over again. Once more the males sang to their mates as they built new nests, incubated. But still no baby birds hatched. One pair tried a third time.

Out of five nests, the finch eggs were one hundred percent sterile.

That same summer, the Song Sparrows and White-crowns were also plagued with problems of sterility. Only about half of their eggs hatched.

Gil and I realized a "silent spring" was beginning in our own backyard.

What was the cause of the birds' troubles? Was it pesticides? If so, the bluebirds would be particularly vulnerable because of their manner of feeding. The blue-bird perches high. As insects drop to the ground, the bird flies down to pick them up. If an insect has been poisoned with a chlorinated hydrocarbon, the bird ab-sorbs the poison, storing it in fatty tissue, where it does not affect the bird immediately.

What about the finches, who are primarily seed eaters? Did they feed in a sprayed field or garden? Or was their problem more complex? Gil had an idea.

"You know, all winter the finches spent more time at the suet feeder than any other birds."

"Could the suet be contaminated?"

"If a steer feeds in a sprayed field," Gil elaborated, "the poison would be stored in the fatty tissue—we call it 'suet.' The animal goes to market before he would use the fat that would have an adverse effect on it."

Is this unhappy situation developing all over the coun-try? The effects are so subtle, often delayed and not im-

mediately discernible. In this busy world, how many
people are aware of what is happening while birds nest,
or when they migrate? How many fall along the way,
unnoticed?

Gil and I had had a long-range plan to go to the Brooks
Range. Our original intention had been to explore the
mountains and try some Arctic mountain climbing. But
six years of intensive bird study and increasing concern
for the vanishing wildlife caused us to change plans. The
mountains would wait. The birds wouldn't.

Through the ages, millions of birds have migrated to
the Arctic to nest. Was the contamination from insecticides extending to the Arctic? Besides exploring Arctic
mountains, we had always wanted to see the fabulous
bird populations of the far north. We could combine the
two plans and still concentrate on the study of contamination in birds.

Lee Rudin, a friend and neighbor, also with an empty
bluebird nestbox, shared our distress about the repro-
ductive problems of birds, and he discussed with us our
concern about the effects of pesticides on birds.

"The U.S. Fish and Wildlife Service," explained Lee,
"is studying this problem. I think Dick Griffith, Chief of
the Division of Wildlife at the Portland office, would like
to hear your story. Maybe there is something you can do
for the Service while you are in the Brooks Range. Why
don't I arrange an interview for you?" Gil and I jumped
at the chance.

Dick Griffith listened sympathetically while we related
what we had observed in our backyard. We expressed
our desire to do something about it.

"I suggest you write to Dr. John Aldrich, Washington,

D.C. He is head of all the research by the Fish and Wildlife Service."

Dr. Aldrich forwarded our letter to D. Glen Crabtree,
Chief, Section of Chemical, Physiological and Pesticide-
Wildlife Studies, Federal Research Center, Denver, Colorado. Mr. Crabtree was responsible for all such studies
conducted west of the Mississippi River.

"We quite agree with you," wrote Mr. Crabtree, "that
these are hazardous times for wildlife and we have some
evidence that pesticides may contaminate northern areas
from 'fall-out' which probably originates from aerial
spray which never reaches the ground at the site in-
tended." Mr. Crabtree then asked us to collect specimens
from Brooks Range, Alaska, for pesticide residue anal-
yses.

The Research Committee of the Mazamas, a mountaineering and conservation organization in Portland,
learned of our plans to collect samples for the U.S.F.W.
and gave us a grant to assist us in our work. The Mazamas also requested some pressed alpine plant specimens from the Arctic for their herbarium.

As our plans progressed, the University of Alaska requested records of birds nesting in the Brooks. Furthermore, they said, their botany department would like
pressed plants from the area.

Our summer's work awaited us.

*   *   *

Gil and I stood apprehensively on the rocky shore of
a desolate wilderness lake in the heart of the Brooks
Range, over 250 airline miles northwest of Fairbanks,
Alaska.

"It looks like the only place to camp is at the north end of the lake," Gil decided.

I looked at the only flat area in the vicinity, 150 yards away.

"There's no protection from the north wind," he added, "but at least it looks level. We haven't much choice."

Then began the job of lugging our 650 pounds of gear and provisions over rough, rocky terrain to our campsite. We had two small tents, tarps, firearms and ammunition, camera equipment, bedding, clothing, cooking equipment with ten gallons of gasoline, and food enough for three months in the wilderness.

Gil carried the cumbersome rifle with each relay. We stayed close together, staggering over uneven stones with enormous loads. Stopping often to look around fearfully, we wondered what was obscured by the sinister shadows. What lay in store for us, two neophytes in this far northern wilderness?

In some knee-high willows, Gil set up our Klepper tent. Driving the pegs he found permafrost just inches below the surface. Our five-and-a-half-foot-high sleeping tent was A-shaped and had only two feet of space beside our air mattress for storage. I stacked our tins of food around the outside, close to the eaves, which for some vague reason gave me a slight feeling of security.

Suddenly we were very tired. Although still daylight, it was midnight.

"What if bears come while we're sleeping?" I asked. I imagined the beasts could be lurking in the willows. "That canvas wouldn't hold back a bear much."

"I've heard that all animals are afraid of smoke." Gil tried to sound convincing. Quickly he gathered up a few dry twigs and made a fire, using a can for a stove.

We crawled into our double sleeping bag on the floor of the tent. The rifle, at the ready, lay near Gil beside our bed. I stared at the wall of the tent and wished I could see through it. Were there any bears out there? Could they scent the smoked dried beef stick hanging over our heads? What was that noise I heard?

Twice Gil got up to check for grizzlies outside, but soon we were weary enough to drop off to sleep.

Chapter II

An Arctic Symphony — and the Concert Hall

Cities give not the human senses room enough.

THE FOLLOWING MORNING, GIL AND I AWOKE IN A SUN-bright tent to a chorus of bird music like nothing we had ever heard before. Hurriedly we dressed to step outside. The Fox Sparrow was one of the miniature musicians, perched on the topmost twig of a willow near our tent, singing with an energy that vibrated his entire little body. A second performer, in a nearby shrub, was not to be outdone. He joined in with equal ardor. His bright rufous cap told us he was an Eastern Tree Sparrow.

Tinkling bird notes were emanating from the grass. "Churrup—churrup—churrup—churrup!" caroled the familiar robin.

In a minor key, a phrase was being executed with pathos by a Gambel's White-crowned Sparrow. In the background a rather colorless trill, all on the same note, by an Arctic Warbler, tied the whole composition together.

But this was more than a quartet. It was an orchestration. Each of the themes was taken up, echoed and re-echoed from the willows throughout the valley, as others of the species proclaimed their territories.

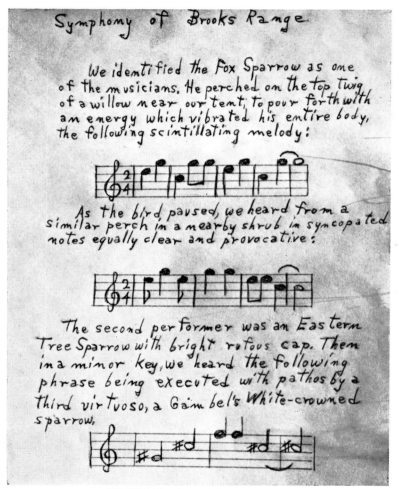

SYMPHONY OF BROOKS RANGE

Music written in the tent while listening to bird songs. The notes were found on a harmonica. The birds answered my imitations of their calls.

WANDERING TATTLER
A slate-gray bird, robin-sized, bobbed and probed with long, dark bill.

The valley was filled with music as the avian perform-
ances continued. Gil and I listened and stood transfixed.
We could understand how Beethoven was inspired to
compose his Pastoral Symphony.

A pair of robin-sized slate gray shorebirds bobbed and
probed with long black bills around gray rocks in a
stream by the camp. "Pa-leep! Paleep!" they called.

"Ah! Those are Wandering Tattlers," exclaimed Gil,
checking Peterson's *Field Guide*. "Few nests of this species have ever been found."

"Maybe we'll find their nest," I offered hopefully.

"Are you kidding? Like looking for a needle in a hay-
stack."

"Their nests were found on the gravel bars, so I'm going to try anyway."

"Don't waste your time. Have you ever searched for

a certain pebble on a beach? That's what the eggs look like—pebbles."

Birds! Birds! Everywhere!

Over our heads, a pair of Arctic Terns hovered with infinite grace to look us over. After spending a southern summer of continuous daylight with the Penguins in the Antarctic, these fragile-looking "sea swallows" had flown here to nest and rear their young in Alaska, again in continuous daylight, at the opposite end of the globe. By flying their yearly round trip of around 22,000 miles, they have no winters, only summers. They spend more time in continuous light and sunshine than any other creatures on earth.

One of the terns settled down on top of a low rounded mound, which formed a peninsula a hundred yards east of camp.

"She's sitting on a nest," Gil announced. "Let's go look at it."

We put on our shoepacs, with rubber bottoms and leather uppers, and waded across a wide creek on slippery rocks to the territory of the terns. Approaching the top of the knoll, we were accosted by frog-like cries. Sharp crimson beaks clicked like castanets to warn us. They wanted no fraternization.

We proceeded anyway. With increasing agitation, both birds swooped down time and again to peck the tops of our hats, knocking them askew. Their ferocity was frightening.

"Ouch! That hurts!" Needle beaks penetrated our hats and pierced our scalps. We cringed, trying desperately to dodge their strikes.

In a slight depression in the firm gravelly soil, we found two eggs—olive with brown markings, the same colors

AN ARCTIC TERN ATTACKING VIVIAN WHEN ITS
NEST WAS THREATENED
The ferocity was frightening

as the sparse vegetation, which was mostly brownish mosses and lichens. Backing off, we were glad to get away from the bad treatment of our peevish neighbors. We had retreated only a few steps when one of the terns settled down on the nest again. The mate resumed hovering over the stream, suspended like a delicate little kite on a short string while peering into the clear water. The terns had already forgotten us.

We had read that the tern mates alternate the incubation. When arriving to change shifts, the returning partner brings its spouse the gift of a fish. We were fascinated with these beauties of striking white plumage, silvery gray mantles and jet black caps. Their short legs and webbed feet matched the vivid red of their beaks.

It took most of the day to establish and organize our wilderness camp. We built a fireplace of stones and

ARCTIC TERN RESTING
Their webbed feet on short legs matched the vivid red of their beaks

gathered sun-bleached driftwood lying around the shore. With great satisfaction, we found that it burned with a clean hot flame. Across the stream a large snowbank— while it lasted—could be our refrigerator. Gil would be cook of our expedition, while I would have a summer of "KP" duties—dishwasher and organizer of food supplies.

Camp was situated on a triangular island delta. A swift icy creek separated into two channels at the head of our island and rushed by on either side of us, gurgling noisily over jumbled gray rocks to empty into Loon Lake. Thus with streams on two sides and the lake on the third, we felt that our "territory" was well defined and we hoped it would be respected by the wildlife.

Dall Mountain Sheep gazed down on us from high ledges on sheer cliffs. Lambs butted heads and played. The ewes lay close by, watching their offspring, contentedly chewing their cuds.

GATHERING SUN-BLEACHED DRIFTWOOD FOR A FIRE
SO THAT GIL COULD BAKE BREAD
My mouth watered at the thought of Gil's specialty, homemade bread prepared with yeast.

Two Rough-legged Hawks soared on effortless wings close to the mountaintops. A raven croaked hoarsely and pursued them. Robins and White-crowns, beaks loaded with insects, were flitting through the bushes, feeding young near camp. Wilson's and Arctic Warblers sang. A Fox Sparrow scratched energetically under a willow. There would never be a dull moment at Loon Lake.

Gil and I were anxious to begin our summer's work. Our first objective was to locate as many bird nests as possible and tag their locations so they could be revisited. We would keep notes on all bird species identified, their activities and abundance of populations. Detailed records would be kept on observations of all wildlife—birds and mammals. Like nosey neighbors, we would pry into their private family affairs.

But there would be as little disturbance to the wildlife as possible. We were here to observe, record and photograph. We hoped to be accepted as part of the wildlife community while we collected plants and gathered samples for DDT analysis.

Eight o'clock that evening we set out on a tour around the lake. Wearing shoepacs, we waded east across the rocky stream. The terns berated us. They were still rude, giving us the "bum's rush" as we hiked past their peninsula.

The ice on the lake, which the night before had been pushed to the south half of the lake, was now in scattered floating cakes being shunted by the wind toward the north end. They were melting rapidly. The slate-gray water reflected the mood of the somber cliffs on the west.

An animal trail led around to the east side where the lower slopes of the mountain eased gently toward the shore. Through shin-high dense shrubs and grass, we found a series of trails, liked plowed furrows in a field, running parallel to the lake. Probably made from caribou migrations, some were smooth and made good traveling.

Beyond, several bands of dense willows, higher than our heads, intercepted our route. Gil carried a .22 revolver but no rifle.

"That pea-shooter will be no good if we run into a grizzly." I eyed the brush ahead. "Let's go down to the shore. It's wide enough to give us a clear view ahead."

"There's no bear around here. We've been here all day and haven't seen a single one. Don't be chicken." Confidently my husband crashed through the willow thickets.

But I was uneasy. Timidly, I crowded close behind

him, bumping into him when I turned to look back. Then willows engulfed us and blocked our vision.

What a relief it was to get back into the open again. Near the trail we flushed an incubating White-crown Sparrow. There were five pretty eggs in her nest, cozily lined with white feathers and concealed in a grass tussock. We tied a small red plastic flag on a twig to mark the location, and hurried on.

"Here's a wolf track!" Gil beamed as he pointed at a muddy place in the trail.

We squatted and studied the big doggy tracks. This elusive meat-eater, true symbol of the wild northland, held a fascination for us. Since reading about Adolph Murie's research on these canines, Gil and I no longer believed in the myth of "the big, bad wolf." The tracks from this lone wolf lent a touch of magic to the whole valley. Since one had traveled here recently, there was a chance we would see a real live wolf.

WOLF TRACK
Tracks of the lone wolf lent a touch of magic to the whole valley

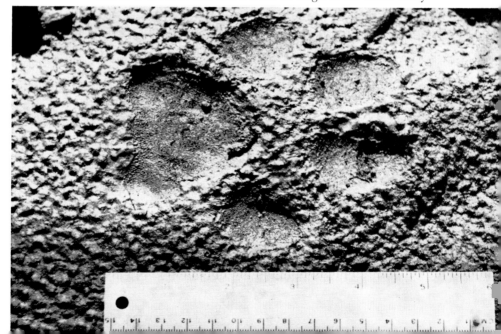

Walking became more difficult as Gil and I proceeded south. The trails seemed to end and we found ourselves struggling through a maze of foot-high cottongrass (*Eriophorum vaginatum*) tussocks. Sticky clay oozed between the clumps and clung heavily to our boots. We moved down to the shore and had easier traveling much to my relief. There we startled Harlequin and Oldsquaw ducks hop-skipping along the rocks.

When halfway to the south end of the lake, a pair of crying Mew Gulls approached. Like bombing planes coming in on a low level run, they flew straight at us, looking as though they meant business. Just when we were eyeball to eyeball, they swooshed up within inches of our heads, spraying us with excrement in their excitement. They kept up this obnoxious procedure with gathering intensity as we walked doggedly on, throwing our arms up to defend ourselves.

We reached the top of a rocky peninsula. While the frenzied gulls swish-swooshed over us, we searched carefully among the rocks but found no nest. Sorry to upset them so, we started to leave. Out of nowhere, a second pair of terns appeared and pandemonium broke loose. The terns, with sharp grating cries, attacked the gulls, which in turn lambasted us. The gulls, larger than the terns, were clumsy in comparison. They mewed and cried piteously while maneuvering to evade the snapping, clicking beaks of the terns.

An hour before midnight we reached the south end of the lake. There was a large jumble of the same kind of gray sedimentary rock as around camp. These, being stabilized, were decorated with black lichens and combined with soil to form another peninsula.

The terns were in a tizzy, now attacking us instead of

the gulls. While they were giving us "the business," a tattler flew up to investigate the commotion. Just a by-stander, it stood watching, not uttering a peep. We searched among the rocks and found the terns' nest on the bare earth and rocks, in almost the same situation as the one near camp. We felt of the two eggs. They were cold—evidence that incubation had not begun.

Using our field glasses, we looked across the water to the gulls' territory and could see clearly where one of the gulls was sitting on a nest on the topmost point of their peninsula. How had we missed it?

The lake had three peninsulas and each was occupied and aggressively defended. There was only one tiny island—about 150 yards from where we stood. The water level of the lake was about fifteen feet below the over-flow outlet at the south end. But we could hear water running through, under the rocks. Two or three hun-dred feet below the rocky rim of the lake, water spouted out. The source of Loon Creek.

Looking over the rim, we saw a wide valley below, filled with brown cottongrass. Far away to the southeast, columns of dark green—almost black—conifers marched for short distances up the slopes on either side of the stream. Treeline was so different from what I had ex-pected.

"What happened to this bush?" I was inspecting a mutilated five-foot-high willow shrub. Branches were broken and shredded, as if beaten and chewed. Bark was skinned off.

"I've heard of 'bear trees.' This could be a 'bear bush'." Gil was looking for tracks.

"Why do they beat it up so?"

"Maybe they're just feeling their oats," Gil mused. "This was done some time ago—probably last year."

The sun shone on the mountains to the east when we headed north toward camp, following the west shore. We kept on the rocks near the water level to avoid more difficult terrain. The steep mountain slope above continued at the same angle right down to the water.

How peaceful to get away from the imbroglio of the harangues and harassments of the terns and gulls.

"What's that? Sounds like a donkey braying. Well, what do you know—it's a bird!" exclaimed Gil. The ridiculous unbird-like calls came from ducks one hundred feet out in the lake. Oldsquaws, three males and one female, swam in single file formation, like children playing follow-the-leader. The weird wild calls and the perpetual daylight made us keenly aware of our wilderness solitude.

Our steps dislodged some rocks which skittered down and slid out of sight in the deep water. We treaded carefully, not wanting to risk a sprained ankle. While we concentrated on each step, two tattlers foraged ahead of us.

"Wouldn't it be great if we could find a tattler nest?" I prattled eagerly. After all, we had already found two tern nests.

"Forget it!" Gil squashed my hopes. "You're licked before you start."

We arrived back at camp after midnight and gulped hot milk drinks. Sleepily we crept into our snug "sack," oblivious to potential danger.

Chapter III

The Honeymooners

No man is quite sane; each has a vein
of folly in his composition.

THE HIGH SUN WARMED OUR TENT AGAIN THE NEXT MORN-
ing and we awoke at nine o'clock. We had overslept,
little dreaming that the drama of this suspense-packed
day would be forever etched in our memories.

We sat out in brilliant sunshine, eating a breakfast of
pancakes and jam and watching the white sheep on the
ledges above camp. Rams were on the west, while ewes
with their frolicking lambs were on the opposite cliffs.
A lamb was having his breakfast too. He waggled his
little tail in ecstasy and butted the ewe's udder. A tern
hovered silently on translucent wings, adding grace and
beauty to the scene. Tranquility reigned over us.

Gil and I began exploring the area around camp. Our
island had many stunted, bushy knee-high willows with
emerging narrow shiny leaves (*Salix glauca*). The tops
were leveled off, as if trimmed with hedge clippers.

"Maybe that's the snow depth in winter," my husband
suggested. "Sheep and caribou could be the hedge trim-
mers. They need to browse on it when lichens and grass
are covered with snow and ice."

An islet in the stream east of us had a half dozen
scraggly eight-foot shrubs with roots anchored in soft
velvety brown moss. These willows, common in Alaska,

have a wide, pale green leaf, dull on the top surface, with whitish fuzz underneath—hence the name Feltleaf Willow *(Salix alaxensis)*.

Thick cushiony brown moss carpeted parts of our island too, but much bare rock and gravel were exposed. Several small saxifrages grew in clumps, decorating some of the rocky areas, along with a few scattered small Horsetails *(Equisetum arvense)*.

After all the tension and hullabaloo of leaving civilization, the peace was heavenly. We were beginning to slow our pace. The warm sun gave us lassitude.

Gil loaded his pack with camera, several lenses and a heavy wooden tripod. My pack was light, with bird and mammal field guides, our record books and a light jacket. We wandered upstream for a couple hundred yards.

Water flowed from beneath a large section of ice that was a quarter mile long and four feet thick. The ice sheet lay on the wide gravel bed of the creek and extended far out over the shore on the east side. We had heard

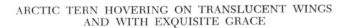

ARCTIC TERN HOVERING ON TRANSLUCENT WINGS
AND WITH EXQUISITE GRACE

about the phenomenon of "overflow" ice in the Arctic. These great sheets of ice, sometimes called "glaciers" by Alaskans, are formed when the stream freezes to the bottom in places. When melting occurs, water flows over the existing ice, where it refreezes and builds up to depths of sometimes eight feet or more. A few streams flow all winter.

Climbing up on the glacier, we walked on smooth, level ice. A half mile north of camp we entered a thicket of ten-foot willows and there was our first Gray-cheeked Thrush nest.

The birds were amazingly tame. A female redpoll stared from her nest in a willow crotch. We had almost missed her. The tiny finch, no larger than Gil's little finger, remained on her nest while he stroked her brown feathers. She turned her head and pecked him! Gil gave the audacious little sprite a gentle nudge. Reluctantly she hopped up a few inches just long enough for us to

REDPOLL NEST IN WILLOW CROTCH
We peeked at five blue eggs nestled in soft white ptarmigan feathers

peek at her five blue eggs nestled in soft white ptarmigan feathers.

We explored thoroughly through the willows, in the branches and on the ground, determined to find every nest. I recorded data on each nest as to species, location, position, contents and any other items of interest. Gil planned to photograph at least one nest of each species, if possible. The camera, with 400mm lens, was mounted on the wooden tripod.

Entranced, we looked down into pink open mouths of three baby robins.

"That would make a good picture," Gil commented. "I'll wait a bit, until the parents feed them." He focused the camera.

"We've found every nest in this thicket," I announced, as I sat down to wait.

The sun grew warmer. I thought about stretching out on the ground for a nap, but we had so much work to do. Moving would keep me awake.

"There's another willow patch a half mile north. Let's go," I urged impatiently.

"Wait a minute. This won't take long," Gil hedged. The parent robin was approaching.

"Why waste time on a robin. They're so common back home." I grew more restless by the minute.

"You go ahead," Gil suggested. "I'll be with you as soon as I get this picture."

"That's suits me. I'll see you in the next thicket."

Swinging my pack on my back, I returned to the creek to get out of the willows and started walking north. The valley extended only a few miles north to the pass. Brush crowded around the stream ahead. Brown grass on either side led up steep slopes to dark cliffs. Tree Sparrows and Whitecrowns scolded me.

I glanced back over my right shoulder. Something moved. I stopped, stunned. By the willow thicket I had just left were two large grizzly bears!

Backlighted by the sun, the bears blended in with the tundra colors. One was light cream color, the other dark brown. I had never seen bears with such big fuzzy heads. Their snouts seemed short and turned up slightly, like a puppy's nose. They were sitting up on their haunches, side by side, cuffing—swinging their big front paws at one another. Oh——they were playing! How charming! They looked so soft and cuddly. Just like two huge Teddy bears.

"Oh, boy!" I thought. "Wait till I tell Gil the good news."

I sneaked back, keeping low, so I would not disturb the bears.

"Guess what I saw—two grizzlies!" I was proud that I had seen them first.

"Where?" Gil jumped up, looking all around the slopes.

"Shh! I'll show you!" I murmured breathlessly. "Be quiet, or they'll hear you."

Gil left his camera with long lenses standing on the tripod. I led him triumphantly to the creek and out of the willows. "There they are!" I pointed back to the bears.

They were sitting where I last saw them, just outside the willow patch, actually only about fifty steps from the camera and the baby robins. At that moment they were closer to the camera than we were.

The two *Ursus horribilis* were still sparring, cuffing each other amiably. This was mating season for grizzlies, and these bears were on their honeymoon. They had attentions only for each other. Honeymooning grizzlies live together for several weeks, mating and affectionately wrestling and playing. The bears didn't even notice us.

"Go get the camera!" I hissed, trembling with excitement. "We'll get some real good pictures. Hurry, while you still have the chance."

"My God! Are you out of your mind?" Gil blurted. "They're dangerous! And I don't even have a gun with me. Come on! Let's go!"

"Don't forget the camera," I rasped, as we started moving.

"I wouldn't go back in that thicket for a million dollars," Gil panted. "Head for camp!"

I was electrified to see Gil's reaction.

"Keep low," Gil demanded. "Don't let them see you. Let's get past the willows!"

With knees bent double and hunched over, we crept, staying in the rocky stream bed. We tried to keep below the knee-high willows on the bank. When the tall willow patch screened us from the bears, we straightened up and bounded off like gazelles. Then we floundered on the rough rocks.

"Let's get on the ice. It's faster!" I vaulted up on the ice, slid and went sprawling.

"Gad! Get back down here," ordered Gil. "They'll see you." He waited only a second.

Bruised and panting, I clambered down off the glacier and dropped into the water. I didn't waste any time. Gil was already leading the way.

"Let's hope those bears don't see us running," Gil puffed. "We wouldn't have a prayer."

I accelerated.

Splashing right down the middle of the stream, we sprinted toward camp. Rocks were slippery. We lurched. We stumbled. We gasped for breath.

Scrambling up the bank of our island, wheezing like steam engines, we finally galloped into camp, too excited even to know we were sopping wet to our hips.

"You keep watch on the grizzlies. I'll get the rifle." Gil disappeared into the tent and was right back out again, loading the rifle.

"There they are. I can see them on the rise, just above the willows." I sat down, trying to catch my breath.

The grizzlies had climbed up a few feet from where we first saw them. They had not noticed us, so intent were they on each other. They shadow-boxed briefly, then shuffled around the rocks on the knoll.

Calming down somewhat, I watched through binoculars. "Hey. This is like a grandstand view," I told Gil excitedly. "Just think. We can watch the mating behavior of grizzly bears. Come here and watch."

Gil was coming to sit beside me.

"Oh-oh. You're too late. There they go, out of sight. They just went down into the willows."

Gil jumped up. "You mean where my camera is?" He grabbed his binoculars but couldn't see the bears.

"Are you sure that's where they went?" Gil didn't want to believe it. He was in anguish at the thought of an entire summer in the wilderness without a camera.

"Yep! That's where they went!"

"Okay," Gil said with determination, "let's try to get the camera."

"You've *got* to be kidding!"

"No. I mean it!"

A little later, we were sneaking back toward the grizzly's willow patch, braver now that Gil was carrying a rifle. I kept close behind him.

Approaching the willows, we nervously crouched beside the glacier in the stream bed, ready to jump at the smallest sound. Gil wanted to circle the willow patch to try to locate the bears, but I was afraid they might come charging out at any minute. Then I had an idea.

"Why don't I climb up the opposite slope a ways and try to see if the camera is all right? You keep between me and the bears."

"Fine. I'll keep in the stream bed between you and the willows."

I began a slow climbing traverse, keeping even with Gil. He followed the edge of the willows. I was jittery and kept looking all around. Soon I was a hundred feet higher than Gil and able to look down on an unreal scene. The willow patch, about two-hundred feet square, was so dense that I could not see into it except at one narrow open area—where the camera should have been. Gil was still sneaking around the edge, peering into the brush, with the rifle in both hands, ready to fire if the bears came rushing out. I could not see the bears or the camera.

Gil glanced up at me and I made a sign that I saw nothing. I climbed higher.

At first, I could see no movement in the brush, but then the darker bear emerged at the far side of the willows and started trotting easily up the slope. I watched the animal stop several times to look back for its cream-colored companion. Gil could not see the bear from his position. He maneuvered with extreme caution farther along the edge of the thicket.

Where was the other grizzly?

I climbed a little higher on the slope. From my new vantage point, I now saw that the camera was still intact on the tripod.

Then Gil noticed the dark bear on the opposite slope. He turned to look up at me, pointing to the bear. I nodded that I saw it.

"Where's the other bear?" he mouthed silently.

I shook my head. Then *a large, furry, cream-colored arm parted the willows.* The huge beast was standing up on his hind legs—right beside the camera. His foot nearly touched the tripod.

"I see him!" I screamed.

Gil froze for a moment, as if bracing for a charge, but neither Gil nor the bear could see each other.

Gil signaled to me, "Where is it?"

I pointed to where the camera was.

The beast raised his nose, as if trying to get our scent. Still standing on its hind legs and looking like a monstrous gorilla, it turned toward the camera. I expected to see it start flailing and wrecking the camera equipment.

But the bear turned again and was obscured by the willows. So far, the camera appeared undamaged.

The bear continued to skulk in the thicket, with Gil stalking it around the perimeter. I could see no activity in the brush. With bated breath, I waited on the slope. Even the birds seemed to be aware of danger. They had hushed their songs. All was quiet.

Then, a crashing in the brush! Horrified, I watched the tops of the willows sway. The grizzly was coming out! In a rush the bear burst into my view—at the back side of the thicket.

"The bear is out! The bear is out!" I screeched. "He's running the other way!"

The cream-colored grizzly galloped off up the slope, following the same path as the other bear. Three mountain sheep scampered to a high ledge and from their safe retreat watched the bear hurrying to join its mate. It disappeared in a gully a mile east of camp.

Gil ran to retrieve the camera.

After our flood of adrenalin had subsided somewhat, we inspected the bird nests and found them undisturbed. The baby robins hid their heads and remained motionless as if anesthetized. The little redpoll eyed us soberly.

Weak and hungry, we trudged back to camp for lunch. As we sat down to rest, Gil heaved a big sigh of relief and he picked up his binoculars.

"My God! There's another grizzly!"

VIVIAN ON LOON PEAK

Below, Tern Peninsula and the north end of Loon Lake. Lower slopes of Ursus in background. Camp in area behind Viv.

Chapter IV

"Old Flakey"

The surprised man of the world is forced to leave his city estimates of great and small, wise and foolish.

ANOTHER GRIZZLY!

"Oh, no! I don't believe I can stand it," I murmured, limp from our last encounter. Weakly, I imitated Gil and focused my binoculars on the mountain slope a mile east of camp.

This bear was cream colored with dark brown face, neck and belly. A panda in reverse. It was foraging on the short vegetation, its great head swinging back and forth. The beast did not move around much. It kept in the same general area, feeding voraciously.

We were famished ourselves and since the grizzly seemed satisfied to continue in that vicinity, we decided to eat lunch while taking turns watching. Never for a moment did we dare take our eyes off it. When we finished eating, the bear was still gorging.

Finally the brute waddled down a few steps to a large outcropping of rock and flopped down. It lay still, flat on its side.

"He's flaked out," Gil announced. "Let's call him 'Old Flakey.'"

With the bear so close, we didn't dare leave camp, in spite of the work to be done.

"You keep watch, and I'll mix up some bread dough," Gil promised. He knew my mouth watered at the thought of his specialty—homemade yeast bread.

The bear was still snoozing. How weird to be working at camp chores with that wild beast sound asleep up there. Blending in with the tundra, he looked as innocent as a lamb, but we knew better and stayed on guard.

Abruptly, the grizzly got up. As we held our breaths, it stretched, turned around, flopped down and went back to sleep.

Once more we relaxed—somewhat.

There was so much work to do, we wanted to get on with it, so we at first began searching for nests near camp, where we found redpolls nesting in the short willows. Venturing west into some taller Feltleaf Willows, we kept watchful eyes on the slumbering grizzly, mindful that other grizzlies could surprise us from any direction. We carried the rifle with us. This was "Operation Alert!"

More nests were located—sparrow, robin, thrush and redpoll. Each was marked with a red plastic flag. We would revisit each one time and again.

There were large bear scats scattered around on the tundra. They contained caribou hair.

"It takes a lot of power to do that!" Gil exclaimed. He was staring at the ground a few yards north of us. My eyes followed his line of vision.

"Ohmygosh!" My hair stood on end.

I stared at a chaotic scene. The tundra had been wildly churned up over a wide area. All the vegetation had been plowed and bulldozed. Shrubs were clawed out—roots in the air. Pieces of caribou hide were scattered throughout. It looked like bulldozers had gone out of control. We had found a "cache," where a grizzly had covered his food. Gil paced it off. It measured thirty feet across. Now we realized the awesome power of the grizzly bear.

Old Flakey! We had forgotten him for a moment! We spun around to check on the sleeping grizzly. Old Rip van Winkle was just getting up. We decided we'd better high-tail it back to camp.

Gil and I settled down for another session of grizzly-watching. The bear began foraging again as if he hadn't eaten for a week. How could he be such a glutton? Then we realized that an animal feeding on vegetation requires more bulk than if it were eating meat. Being omnivorous, bears eat both.

Old Flakey was relishing his salad. He foraged back and forth, working steadily downhill, closer to camp. We became increasingly alert. With anxious glances over his shoulder, Gil started supper.

The grizzly must have scented our tracks from the trip on that side of the lake. All of a sudden he started running our way, nose to the ground. We prepared for action—in case he wanted some meat. Gil grabbed the rifle and checked to see if it was loaded. Then he raced to get the shotgun.

"Here. You take it!" He handed the gun to me. "Do you know how to work it?"

"No."

"Quick! Here's how."

"The camera!" Gil sprinted for the camera.

Abruptly, the bear stopped dead in his tracks in a low thicket and began grazing. Some delicacy had proved irresistible.

The grizzly had come halfway.

With nerves tight as bowstrings, we watched Old

Flakey, his hulking tan back moving back and forth in the thicket. Suddenly, with nose to the ground, the grizzly was galloping toward us again. We were staring death in the face.

For an instant I was paralyzed, my feet glued to the ground.

"Make a big noise. Make a big noise." I flew for the frypan.

The bear raced into a gully on the opposite side of Tern Peninsula and was hidden behind the tern's knoll.

Gil held the camera ready, rifle beside him. In a trance, eyes glued on the knoll, I held the shotgun. Close at hand—a frypan and spoon—to make big noise! In a moment the beast would come charging over the top!

We watched.

And listened.

No sound. No bear!

A tern sat silently on the nest. I saw it look around and centered my attention on it. The tern would give the alarm.

Gil muttered under his breath.

"What did you say?" I asked in a hushed voice.

"Do you know that a grizzly has been clocked at thirty-five miles an hour?"

We waited.

"He could be here in less than half a minute," Gil calculated.

Then we saw him—on the other side of Tern Peninsula, grazing, moving slowly the other way. *We felt like victims of a monstrous cat-and-mouse game.*

Still watching, we gulped coffee to settle our nerves. Now we knew why grizzlies were called unpredictable.

Old Flakey kept foraging, moving slowly up the slope

away from us. A half mile away, he was still gorging. We grabbed a bite of supper.

Gil proceeded with working down the bread dough while we kept our eyes peeled for Old Flakey—or any other grizzly. For many long hours, the bear foraged on the slope, moving erratically, until at nine P.M. he disappeared up into the same gully the "Lovers" had gone— the one we called "Lover's Gully." At long last, we were at ease.

"What's that?" Gil asked sharply, looking behind me.

Out of the corner of my eye, I saw a large tan object coming toward us. I jerked around and stared wide-eyed at a caribou doe. At that precise moment, the creature saw us, turned, and fled north. She looked so lonesome running up the valley with her peculiar gait. A curious clicking sound came from her enormous hooves as her rear legs swung outward. Nevertheless, she was elegantly graceful.

At ten p.m. I was in the tent working on records. Gil let out a yell.

I exploded out of the tent. "What is it?"

"Look at the beautiful bread!" Gil was celebrating his achievement.

"Please don't do that to me. Don't yell like that, if you want me to survive the summer. I'm a nervous wreck."

But that bread was indeed beautiful. And, since Gil and I had been without bread for many days—our fare had been pancakes, which were running out our ears— we set to and devoured half a loaf of the delicious bread without stopping.

When getting ready for bed, we had "grizzly drill."

Gil practiced a quick draw—with a cumbersome rifle in the close quarters of our little tent.

"If I have to use this," Gil advised, "you'd better duck out of the way. Get under the sleeping bag."

I hung the frypan over our heads and had a big spoon handy. Who would win out in an emergency, the bear or us?

It took me a long time to get to sleep that night. Two or three times I went out to look around with binoculars. Then I went back to bed, where Gil was already fast asleep.

We love life, I thought. What are we doing here anyway? I prayed.

"LOOK AT THE BEAUTIFUL BREAD!"
Gil was celebrating his achievement

Chapter V

Semi-Arid Desert?

*Every rational creature has all nature
for his dowry. It is his, if he will.*

THE MORNING OF JUNE 30TH, I AWOKE, SURPRISED WE WERE
still alive. We spent a long time carefully glassing the
slopes with binoculars. Gil watched several tan colored
hummocks to see if they moved. There was small comfort from being on an island. Grizzlies could cross the
streams faster than we could. We looked at the Feltleaf
Willow patch west of camp, wishing it were farther
away.

But the rifle no longer stayed in the tent. Now it
rested beside the fireplace while Gil prepared his omelet
recipe for breakfast.

Ready to leave camp for a day's hike, loaded packs on
our backs, we saw Old Flakey appear on the slope again.

"Oh, no!" I wailed. "Not the old cat-and-mouse game
again!"

The grizzly had spent the night in the gully close by.
Had we known, we would have kept an all-night vigil.

We put down our packs, ready to protect the camp.

The bear foraged on the slope again. Once he clawed
around some boulders, moving large rocks with appalling
ease.

"Just like a bulldozer," I thought out loud as we stared
in awed fascination.

On guard every minute, we worked around camp. Old Flakey began ranging north and at noon he finally disappeared from view about one mile from camp.

"Hey! It's raining!"

Big drops spattered on the tins. We looked up. Dark clouds boiled over the peaks. Engrossed with grizzly watching, we had not noticed a storm brewing. As we scurried to cover our supplies with plastics, a north wind came up, then rain beat down in earnest.

"The storm won't last long. It doesn't rain much in the Arctic," Gil stated. "We'd better not go in the Klepper. Have to keep watch. That bear could be back any minute."

For an hour we huddled under a plastic tarp—in a miserable cold rain. Temperature, 37°.

"*The Arctic is a semi-arid desert,*" Gil expounded. "*Not much rain. Be prepared for heat in the summertime.*"

My amateur explorer husband had read extensively to prepare us for our Arctic adventures. We had brought no rain garments, thinking we'd use light tarps for infrequent showers.

Our plan had been to cook out in the open. The sleeping tent would be too crowded and our other tent was a low two-man mountain tent for backpacking.

There had been ample warnings about "unbelievable" swarms of voracious mosquitoes, so I had sewed an eight-foot square "tent" of mosquito netting. With that, we could cook and eat in comfort—we had hoped. So far, the prepared-for mosquitos were no problem, but the rain was.

The shower ended as abruptly as it had started.

We were impatient to get on with the delayed hike

to search for more nests. At the same time, we could check on the bear's whereabouts.

North of camp, we were met by a caribou doe with a rather small fawn. We stood stock-still. The parent *Rangifer arcticus* was light brown, wore a slightly tousled white cape, and had a distinctive brown mark over her nose. She gazed at us, as if with disbelief, her large luminous dark eyes measuring us. Her ears cocked forward beneath short brown velvety antlers. The sensitive soft muzzle quivered, sniffing danger. Rear legs were braced apart, taut as wound steel springs. Her whitish long-legged fawn stood hesitantly some yards behind, awaiting her decision.

Like a flash, the spell was broken. The doe wheeled and fled. Up the slope she skimmed, with her youngster following closely at her heels. They sprang up Lover's Gully, where Old Flakey had gone. Shortly thereafter, we were surprised to see the two nimble deer on a pre-

CARIBOU DOE
She gazed at us as if with disbelief, her large, luminous, dark eyes measuring us.

cipitous knife ridge. Had they encountered the grizzly?

Traveling north for several miles, Gil and I were caught in a downpour that soaked us to the skin. To add to our discomfort, we found ourselves floundering in a large field of cottongrass tussocks. We entertained thoughts of going back to camp.

Then, in the bushes and on the ground we found some more nests. With new life, we played our game, Who could find the most nests? Eagerly, we prowled through some spindly Feltleaf willows, close to Grizzly Grove (where we had encountered the Lovers). We moved with caution, listening, watching for bears. I was as tense as a cat stalking a mouse. On a small island, I leaned over, and a gray form exploded in my face!

"Gad!" My heart stopped.

A small gray Harlequin duck had flushed from her nest, not two feet from me. She slipped quickly into the water and vanished downstream. Six creamy eggs, the size of chicken eggs, lay in a fluffy nest of gray down— hidden in grass under a leaning willow. With feelings of guilt in spite of the good cause, we collected one of her precious eggs for a DDT analysis then made a hasty retreat so that she could return to her nest.

After finding the Harlequin nest, I waded across the icy stream with reckless abandon, hoping to find more duck nests, ignoring the water flowing over my boot tops. With each step ice water squished inside my boots, but in my excitement I didn't feel the cold.

The shrill plaintive "Pa-leep, paleep" of the tattlers spurred us on to searching for their nests. They seemed to be defending territories at several places along the gravel bars.

"I'll bet if we ever do find a tattler nest, the bird won't utter a sound," Gil speculated.

Although we found no tattler nest, we found a number of redpoll, thrush, robin and Tree Sparrow nests and collected some dead young birds from them.

In a cold rain we arrived back at camp, shivering and wet from head to toes. My feet were like ice. After changing into dry warm clothing, Gil went out in the wind and rain to cook supper. I put my feet into the sleeping bag and caught up with nest records. Soon my feet were toasty warm.

"Supper is ready!" Gil called.

I went out. He had contrived a makeshift shelter of plastic supported by sticks, and we were able to sit out of the wind and rain. That hot food tasted better than any banquet in civilization. It was all we asked for at the moment.

Rain drummed steadily on the tent most of the night as we snuggled deep in our sleeping bag.

July 2nd. It began to snow as we sat watching our fourth grizzly rummaging for roots on the mountainside east of camp. This bear was dark brown on most of the back half of his body and light colored around the front. His fur was whitish on his head and around the top of his rump. He looked as though he had been ransacking a flour barrel.

The grizzly kept busy digging and feeding, traversing first one way, then another, about halfway up the slope. For several hours we mounted guard, until the beast finally vanished into the snowy mists.

Since we had seen all four grizzlies on that mountain, we named it "Ursus Peak."*

The first few days of July had temperatures near freezing, with snow turning to steady rain in the valley. But snow frosted the peaks down to a thousand feet above us and the north wind blew incessantly. The weather was so miserable, we decided to build a shelter for cooking.

Willow poles and driftwood, collected around the shore, made a frame over which we stretched a heavy plastic anchored by poles driven into the ground. Built behind the stone fireplace and open on the south side, the shelter was a snug haven when the wind and rain blasted us from the north. The plastic allowed us to watch for grizzlies approaching from the back.

Adjacent to the cook shelter we constructed a small extra shelter of plastic for firewood, which we gathered in sufficient quantities to keep a constant supply dry enough to burn.

While I contrived a table and seats from boxes, Gil prepared the specimens for air-drying. Dead young birds were split open and spread out on plywood, while eggs were opened on a plastic plate to dry. Most of the eggs we collected were ones that had been incubated but had not hatched. The samples were kept in the tent when the weather was bad and moved out in the sun whenever possible.

Every waking moment, we were on guard for grizzlies. When we went to bed, we were tired enough to sleep. Sort of playing Russian Roulette, Eskimos told us later. They have dogs to watch while they sleep.

---

*The name has been accepted by State and National Boards on Geographic Names.

GIL CARRYING FIREWOOD ACROSS THE CREEK TOWARD CAMP
We gathered it in sufficient quantities to keep a supply dry enough to burn

It was still raining when we hiked around the lake again—this time carrying the rifle, now our constant companion. We made other short sorties in the blowing rain. By dressing warmly, we were comfortable while hiking, but it was a real luxury to return to the plastic shelter after several days of cooking and eating in wintery weather. In the wilderness, such simple conveniences gave us far more pleasure than had all the material possessions of civilization. Living primitively as we were and beginning to develop a feeling of accomplishment, we experienced a keener enjoyment of life—all life.

Little baby birds, out of the nests, were crying on both sides of camp. I was worried for their safety away from their snug feather-lined nests, but none of the species seemed perturbed by the foul weather. We still heard the sweet music of the White-crown and Tree Sparrow. A Wheatear flew down to forage around camp when his nest area on the upper slopes became covered with snow.

We enjoyed the terns for neighbors. Delicately graceful as they silently hovered and skimmed over the streams close by, they were a never-ending source of delight. When their peninsula was not violated, all was serene. Both terns and tattlers were adjusting to our presence. They had their territories and we had ours.

The sheep, always visible on the cliffs above us, were accepting us, too, as part of their community. They moved ever lower and closer to our camp. We watched one of the sheep come down the east cliffs and descend until it was almost to the valley floor. It stood hesitant for a half hour, gazing around from a low bank. Finally, the sheep dashed down into the willows near the creek. In no time, it was across on the other side, sprinting

THE SHEEP WERE ACCEPTING US, TOO, AS PART
OF THE COMMUNITY
They moved ever lower and closer to camp

up the west banks toward the cliffs on the opposite side of the valley. It had crossed the valley floor at the narrowest place.

Gil caught a glimpse of a Snowshoe Hare in the Felt-leaf Willow patch west of camp. Later we found all that remained of one—a rabbit foot quite dried up. We saw no others of the species while at Loon Lake.

Wilson's Warblers, little bits of yellow sunshine, had their nest of infinitely small young hidden in a clump of grass just outside a thicket.

One day it rained so hard we stayed in camp all day. Frustrated by the intolerable weather and with the chill adding zest to our appetites, we turned our thoughts to food. Gil decided to try pizza, but he could not get the reflector oven hot enough. He contrived another kind of oven, opening the end of a square five-gallon gasoline can with a can opener and placing it directly over a roar-

GIL CAUGHT A GLIMPSE OF A SNOWSHOE HARE IN THE
FELT-LEAF WILLOW PATCH WEST OF CAMP
Later we found all that remained of the snowshoe—a rabbit foot

GIL COOKING AT OUR PLASTIC SHELTER

ing fire. This worked perfectly. We were soon smacking our lips over savory hot pizzas.

We discovered that water had leaked into the tin containing the bouillon packages and tea bags.

"I'll dry the bouillon, if you'll dry the tea bags," Gil challenged with a grin. He knew he had the better bargain.

With a towel, he started drying nearly a hundred metal foil packages of bouillon. I was amused, until I began trying to disentangle the strings of as many tea bags— without squeezing any of the water out. I wanted to save as much flavor as possible. But the strings were inextricably knotted. Gil was finished when I gave up in despair. I finally hung the whole hopeless mess on a line in the tent and spread a plastic to catch the drippings.

Ears in the wilderness that rainy evening must have been startled into alertness at the strange sounds of two

FRUSTRATED BY THE MISERABLE WEATHER, OUR
THOUGHTS TURNED TO FOOD
Shown here: doughnuts without holes

Homo sapiens laughing uncontrollably at the ludicrous
sight of one hundred stained, wet tea bags hanging over
their bed.

Chapter VI

Studies in Contrasts

> *How easily we walk onward into the
> opening landscape, absorbed by new
> pictures and new thoughts.*

THE RAINS STOPPED ON THE 4TH OF JULY. TO CELEBRATE
the day, we planned an all-day hike. The clouds broke up
and the warm sun made our spirits soar. Gil led the way
north, loaded with camera, lenses and big wooden tripod. With a long strap over my shoulder, I carried the
heavy rifle, the bolt of which bumped my hip at every
step. I was gun-bearer, ready to hand him "Big Bertha"
quickly in an emergency. On shortened straps, our binoculars swung around our necks at all times. We found
this the most comfortable and convenient way to carry
them and still to have them immediately accessible.

Tree Sparrows and White-crowns, beaks crammed
with insects, scolded us every step of the way. Now and
then, a Savannah Sparrow joined in. We had not gone
far when we were confronted by an incredibly brave
Semipalmated Sandpiper defending two downy young.
We were two Gullivers facing a Lilliput as she stood her
ground just two feet from us.

Off the valley floor, shrubs were short. Willows com-
peted with a prostrate Labrador Tea *(Ledum decum-
bens)* and Dwarf Birch *(Betula nana)*. This birch has

small round leaves and hugs the ground to survive the rugged climate.

We entered a narrow gorge where rippling waterfalls splashed down a rocky staircase. Great chunks of ice clung to the stony cliffs, suspended over the cascading waters. Mingled with the music of the falling waters, were tinkling flute-like notes emanating from the cool mossy depths. Then we saw a dumpy-looking gray bird perched on the edge of the ice pouring his heart out in an enchanting melody. A Water Ouzel. Also called the Dipper, this bird is the water sprite which bobs in deep-knee bends, then walks on the rocks into the stream. He flies right through the water as easily as through the air, as though water and air were one medium.

These intriguing creatures are resident here the year around. At isolated places where open water can be found, even in the heart of the frigid Arctic winter, the delightful Dipper will merrily survive.

The little water nymph sang his dulcet notes again, then vanished in the swirling waters.

Following a small stream, we climbed up into a narrow canyon. With our visibility limited, we were playing a dangerous game. Signs of bear were everywhere. Gil led warily around each blind corner. Close at his heels, I was rear guard.

Two magnificent Buteo Hawks, one nearly all white, swung out over towering cliffs. Riding the updrafts on widespread pinions, they soared effortlessly out of sight. Later, when we came out of the canyon at a 3,500-foot elevation, we looked down into the Rough-legs' aerie. Four white eggs, two faintly splotched with tan, lay in a coarse stick nest thickly lined with grass. While I be-layed him with a light line, Gil descended to collect an

VIVIAN LOOKING FOR A WATER OUZEL NEST
We heard the beautiful song of the water ouzel, then spotted it perched on
the ice above a waterfall.

ROUGH-LEGGED HAWK'S NEST

Four white eggs, faintly splotched with tan, in a stick nest thickly lined
with grass.

ROUGH-LEGGED HAWK

The bird hovered over us with soft, complaining cries which evoked more
sympathy than the aggressiveness of the gulls and terns.

egg. The worried hawks circled over our heads, uttering soft complaining cries. They were not aggressive and their plaintive calls evoked more sympathy than had the fierce attacks of the terns and gulls.

Hurriedly we left the disturbed Raptores and went over a rounded ridge to get out of their line of vision. We sat down to watch a male Wheatear with a black bandit mask feeding two appealing fat, fuzzy, stubby-tailed young. They bobbed as they stared at us unafraid and made a buzzing sound, like a Jew's harp note, to keep in contact with their parents.

We saw our first Golden-crowned Sparrow of the area. To our knowledge, no nest of this species had been found in the Brooks Range.* The bird scolded briefly, then flitted below into some willows, where we heard its plaintive three-note whistle, "Three Blind Mice."

---

*Gil and I found three Golden-crowned Sparrow nests at the heads of the Unakserak and Kutuk Rivers, summer 1968.

WHEATEAR CHICK
The stubby-tailed young creature stared at us unafraid. The bird makes a buzzing sound like a Jew's harp note.

Gil and I sat on cushions of soft and lovely lichens, soaking up the warm sun. The creamy three-dimensional lace called "Reindeer Moss" (*Cladonia rangiferina*), of which there were several varieties, covered the soil in some places between the rocks to depths of several inches. When moistened with rain, the lichens are a springy carpet of unimaginable elegance. But when dry, they are so delicate and fragile that the slightest pressure shatters them into a million pieces. We hated to crush them with our boots.

There was an interesting brown and silver lichen (*Cetraria richardsonii*) which resembled miniature staghorns. It lay curled up in rows, loose from the ground, tossed about by the winds. Having no roots, it receives its sustenance only from the atmosphere.

The rocks on the ridge were unbelievably beautiful, like gorgeous abstract paintings, decorated by flat lichens. Some rocks were covered in brilliant hues of orange

CETRARIA RICHARDSONII

It lay curled up in rows, loose from the ground, tossed about by the winds.
Having no roots, it receives its sustenance from the atmosphere.

and red, others in more subdued tones of chartreuse and yellow. Still others held designs in gray—even white— and black.

"To speak truly," wrote Emerson, "few adult persons can see nature. In the presence of nature, a wild delight runs through the man." We saw it now. We felt it.

There was so much loveliness in the detail of the tundra and rocks that at times there was just too much beauty to absorb. To rest my senses I let my eyes stray across the valley and over the slopes in the distance where there was a plainness and lack of color.

Working eastward, we came upon a wide plateau at 3,500-foot elevation. No willows here except "Snow Willows" (there are several species), which lay prostrate on the ground, and other stunted shin-high species in shallow draws. These plains were nearly flat, with peaks on the south and the Ekokpuk Valley on the north. The land looked desolate. Brown and apparently lifeless, it seemed like the end of all creation. These were the barrens.

We found excellent walking on firm gravelly soil—dry tundra—with vegetation an inch or two high. There was grass, too, and other plants, but all were short. And lakes, with ice around the border. And animal life. Birds migrate to this austere highland to nest. There were elegant Long-tailed Jaegers, hawking over territories of Lapland Longspurs, Horned Larks and Savannah Sparrows nesting on the flats.

We circled a small lake while two female Harlequins and a Red-breasted Merganser swam in comical single-file formation a stone's throw away. With wakes like tiny motor boats, the two Harlequins kept pace with us, in a smaller circle, as we hiked around the shore.

THE LAND LOOKED DESOLATE, LIKE THE END
OF ALL CREATION

We found excellent walking on dry tundra, with vegetation an inch or two
high.

We came upon a family of Snow Buntings. The plump
young, still unable to fly, ran in and out of the lichen-
covered rocks to be fed. The busy parents had abso-
lutely no fear of us as they crammed insects into de-
manding young throats.

Rosy Finches nested in crevices at lakeside, and the
elusive Golden-crown was carrying food for young.
Mew Gulls nested there, and a Baird's Sandpiper de-
coyed.

All these species had chosen to nest in this inhospitable
habitat. All were in a frenzy of reproducing quickly,
because summer is so brief—only a few short weeks.

We called these the "Snow Bunting Lakes."

We lingered awhile, loafing on the sun-warmed rocks,
watching fat lazy white fluffs of clouds drifting over the
peaks.

SNOW BUNTING LAKE
Elevation, 3,500 feet, with ice around the border

SILHOUETTE OF LONG-TAILED JAEGER
They hawked over the territories of the birds nesting in the barrens

MEW GULL NEST AT 3,500 FEET ELEVATION
Near an alpine lake, with *Anemone parviflora* blooming beside it

GIL LOOKING FOR SCULPINS AT SNOW BUNTING LAKES
He is using a caribou antler

Anemone narcissiflora. Over-size Bumblebees, dressed in black and yellow velvet were working on the flowers.

Andromeda polifolia. Only one inch tall, all their delicate pink bells faced the same direction.

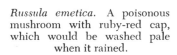

Russula emetica. A poisonous mushroom with ruby-red cap, which would be washed pale when it rained.

Arctostaphylos alpina. Bear-berry grew on the knolls around camp. In August, leaves turned to burgundy.

Aster sibericus. Siberian Aster grew in sandy locations along Loon Creek.

Saxifraga escholtzii. A quarter-inch thick mat decorated rocks in a sheltered nook. Twin pistils identified it as a saxifrage.

Hedysarum alpinum. We found bright pink Vetch blooming like unfurled flags on a staff.

Polemonium acutiflorum. Delicate blue Jacob's Ladder in profusion under Feltleaf Willows.

WE CIRCLED A SMALL LAKE WHILE TWO FEMALE HARLEQUINS
SWAM A STONE'S THROW AWAY
With wakes like tiny motorboats, they kept pace with us

We were no more than started toward "home" when
we noticed some small birds ahead engaged in a fidgety
feathered flurry of excitement. They were venting their
righteous wrath on a dainty little furred creature darting
around the rocks. An ermine (*Mustela erminea arctica*),
in summer coat of rich golden brown and creamy white,
hunted to the accompaniment of Longspurs and pipits in
a frenzy of chirping expletives. With lithe sleek grace,
the weasel skipped over our way, then stretched up on
delicate white toes. For an instant an earnest little face
scrutinized us with burning curiosity. In a twinkling it
vanished among the lichen-decorated rocks.

A Yellow Wagtail, from Asia, foraged in the short vegetation when we made our way across the rounded hills,
taking a shortcut toward camp. Emerging from a gully,

ERMINE

For an instant an earnest little face scrutinized us with burning curiosity

WITH LITHE SLEEK GRACE, THE WEASEL SKIPPED OVER OUR
WAY, THEN STRETCHED UP ON DELICATE WHITE TOES

we could see our lonely camp a few miles away, at the
edge of the hourglass lake.

Angling down the slope, photographer leading with
gun-bearer behind, we were brought up abruptly by another grizzly "cache." The bulldozed area looked as
though two prehistoric monsters had been engaged in a
life-and-death struggle. The scene of turmoil was strewn
with caribou hide and hair. Antlers of a large bull barely
protruded from the convulsed earth. Fresh large bear
scats containing caribou hair lay scattered over the tundra. Since visibility was restricted on one side of us, we
knew that one of the fearsome beasts could be down on
us without warning. Like two scared rabbits, we lost no
time in scramming out of there.

Down the hill, we felt safer as we neared camp. Traversing a couple hundred yards above the stream on a

GIL AT SNOW BUNTING LAKES
We lingered awhile, basking on the warm rocks

section of caribou trail, Gil led the way across a gentle slope strewn with black-lichen-covered rocks.

"Well, I'll be——! A TATTLER NEST!" Gil whooped.

He had been about to step on an incubating tattler when the gray bird slipped off the nest without uttering a sound. Not until it had flown down to the stream did it begin its plaintive shrill calls.

We danced with glee. Not only had we made a rare find, but the nest was in a different habitat than expected. All the tattlers making a fuss down on the gravel bars could be nesting up on the slopes.

"Let's come back tomorrow to get a picture of the tattler on a nest." Gil was jubilant over the prospect of this rare opportunity.

Carefully, we marked the location with a red plastic flag on either side, equidistant from the nest. Further, we placed a conspicuous lichen-covered rock beside it.

WE LOOKED DOWN AT THE HOURGLASS LAKE
Overflow ice at the lower right

Going by Grizzly Grove (the Lovers' thicket) we found our first fledgling robin of the season. Checking some nests, we collected some more dead young birds and unhatched eggs.

With ravenous appetites, we trudged into camp. For several days I had been urging Gil to serve noodles with sour cream sauce made from a package mix. I'm very fond of sour cream sauce, but he prefers other food and had always managed to resist my request. Tonight, however, just to please me, he was going to make this *pièce de resistance*. My mouth watered.

In the Klepper, I worked on records until I heard his happy call, "Come and get it!"

As I emerged from the tent, I was surprised to see storm clouds threatening.

"Get it while it's hot!" my chef urged cheerily, dishing up the meal.

"That cloud on Ursus Peak looks like a wind cloud," I announced worriedly. A sudden gust of wind crackled the plastic on the shelter.

"Come on, it's cooling off," Gil was impatient and sat down to eat. "Here's your sour cream sauce."

"I know my wind clouds. I'm from Kansas. Batten down the——"

At that precise moment, a blast from the south hit the shelter that had been designed for north winds. It bellowed out like a sail.

Gil was unperturbed. He started to eat.

Another blast of wind. I grabbed for the front of the shelter.

"Help!" I screeched.

Pots, lids, cans, jackets, specimens and sundry articles started flying all around us. Gil staggered up to help me as I struggled to keep hold of the top edge of the shelter. The Coleman stove tipped, water spilled, boxes

WE WERE BROUGHT UP ABRUPTLY BY ANOTHER
GRIZZLY "CACHE"
Antlers of a large bull protuded from the convulsed earth

tumbled. The plastic snapped and whipped, then it was clawed out of our hands. The shelter flew off with the wind.

Everything was a shambles. The shelter stretched out to the north—with food, boots, dishes, utensils, scattered through the low willow shrubs. At first we were too shocked to say anything. Our lovely shelter gone in an instant. Possessions scattered over the whole island.

"Our beautiful shelter!" I sobbed.

Then came a deluge of rain! With wind!

I began to laugh hysterically and couldn't stop. It was the funniest thing I had ever seen—noodles and sour cream sauce scattered over the bushes and the ground, in the rain. A Kansas tornado had just gone through.

Laughing wildly, hair streaming, clothes whipping in the wind, I started tossing things up in the air to add to the chaos.

"Quick!" Gil came suddenly to life. "Record books! Specimens—in the rain!" He screamed, trying to get me

A WANDERING TATTLER'S NEST ON A MOUNTAIN SLOPE TWO HUNDRED YARDS FROM UPPER LOON CREEK

to come to my senses. "Your glasses are somewhere—and our binoculars!"

I sobered up. For a moment I stared at the tipped can of powdered potatoes, contents spilled out on the ground. Gil was racing around, picking up record books, specimens, dashing to put them in the Klepper. Back out to find both binoculars. I swung into action. In the wind and rain, we scrambled through the wreckage, salvaging what dried food had not spilled. Gil scooped up some cooked noodles from the ground and I scraped up a little sour cream sauce from a piece of plastic. We gulped some (along with bits of lichen and willow leaves) while we raced through the shrubs, searching and finding, throwing things under tarps, tossing them in the Klepper.

We retrieved what we could but didn't stop there. We started rebuilding the shelter. Poles were put back up, spliced, wired. The torn plastic was salvaged, patched, taped and tied with surgical tape. Later, I finally found my prescription colored glasses under the bushes. Unbroken, thank God! The hawk egg specimen was safe in a plastic cup with an air-tight lid.

From my diary.
At eleven p.m. we had the shelter back together again. We gathered up what food we could—mashed potatoes, scattered powdered milk. Cleaned up the mess as best we could. Washed up the dishes and utensils. At midnight, Gil prepared another supper. Instant mashed potatoes and canned meatballs.

Then we went to bed. We were a little tired.

Chapter VII

Post Office Ursus, and an Ego Restored

Nature stretcheth out her arms to embrace man. . . .

THE LILTING SONG OF THE FOX SPARROW WOKE US IN THE morning. What a happy sound. Tree Sparrow and White-crown joined in. A gentle rain tapped the tent.

Robins were feeding young near camp when Gil got up to fix breakfast. A pair of Golden Eagles soared over Ursus. I stayed in bed awhile to write.

Most of the forenoon, we worked at reinforcing and anchoring the shelter. Larger poles strengthened it, heavy rocks and guy ropes anchored it. In the afternoon, we watched as ominous dark storm clouds moved closer. Wind blew from the north while the storm approached from the south. We scurried to further brace the shelter. Fastening a tarp to the front of the frame, we anchored it to the heavy rocks on the ground, hoping to deflect a south wind.

Suddenly, the wind switched. Wind and rain again slammed us from the south. Gil and I stood inside the shelter, bracing our backs against the tarp, while the wind pushed in. We clung to the top edge of the shelter frame, hanging on once again as the wind pressed harder against us. Harder—harder the wind blew. The shelter creaked and shuddered, and our fingers ached from the strain. But we kept clinging desperately.

Then it was all over. The shelter held.

The weather brightened as the storm continued up the valley. Then it was beautiful. We made our way north to photograph the tattler nest. The rock-strewn slope was wider than we recalled, but at last, Gil spotted one of the red plastic flags, nibbled by some small creature. Neither the tattler nor the nest could be seen. We found the other flag and lined up the two as we had planned. Still we could not find the nest. Finally, by using binoculars, we closely scrutinized midway between the two flags until we saw the rock with the colorful lichen that we had placed beside the nest. We examined carefully where the nest was supposed to be.

The tattler was there! A gray bird on a gray nest amid gray rocks. Not a feather moved. Only a quick flick of an eyelid.

THE TATTLER WAS THERE!
She looked for all the world like another gray rock. Not a feather moved, and there was only the faintest flick of an eyelid.

What a marvelous camouflage! When photographing the bird, Gil had a hard time finding it in the viewer. No wonder few tattler nests have ever been found.

The following day we returned and the nest was empty. Tattlers pa-leeped down by the stream.

"Two days later and we never would have found a tattler nest," Gil commented. "How lucky can you get!"

July 6th, that same day, three fluffy round balls of gray and white fuzz—golf ball size—ran on twinkling wire-like legs around the stream near camp. A pair of adult tattlers watched solicitously over them, guarding from the shore, but mostly while perched in the willows. With pa-leeps, they called their offspring together whenever they strayed too far. (Not until they had young to guard did we see tattlers calling from the top willow branches.)

The swift water was no handicap for the downy young. They bobbed and probed with short black bills, foraging

TATTLER CHICK A FEW DAYS OLD
A fluffy round ball of gray and white fuzz—golf ball size

TATTLER DOWNY YOUNG A FEW DAYS OLD
He bobbed upon his toes in a dainty little curtsy

in the shallows, swimming across the stream like ducklings.

The islet with the Feltleafs, in the stream just east of camp, held a surprise for us. A robin had kept her nest a secret while watching our camp activities. Across from where we had been getting water, she nested two eggs and one new young, low in a willow crotch—practically under our noses.

Gil is an ardent fisherman. We had not brought enough meat for our stay in the wilderness and planned to supplement with fish. We knew there were fish in the lake, because we had watched the terns catch small silvery slivers and gulp them down. Gil eagerly assembled his fishing gear to try his luck. Not a strike. Not biting that day.

Another day, Gil took out his gear and cast again.

ROBIN'S NEST, WITH CHICK JUST HATCHED
On the tiny islet just east of camp. The parent had been incubating "right under our noses" without our being aware of it.

Still not a single strike. He watched the terns catching fish in the riffles. If there were small ones, there should be larger ones. What kind were they?

Again and again, Gil cast out. In vain. A tern carried another fish to its mate. Gil's *homo sapiens* ego was beginning to suffer.

With his 20-20 vision, the frustrated fisherman began watching the shallows. Although he could not spot any fish, he watched a tern pick up another fingerling from the other side of our island. Gil began spending much time gazing into the shallow water, obsessed.

"Let's travel south," he suggested one evening. "That stream down below the rim of the lake may have some fish."

We loaded up with our usual paraphernalia plus the fishing gear and at 10:30 p.m. waded east across the stream. The tattlers were chasing the terns and gulls away from the streams around our island, appropriating the territory for their unconcerned downy chicks, who were busy with their constant probing in the water and mud.

Three Rock Ptarmigan erupted from the grass when we hiked on a caribou trail east of the lake.

At the gulls' peninsula, it was bedlam again. A downy gull chick swam far out on the lake, and the parents noisily took turns flying over it protectively as it rocked up and down the waves, bobbing like a cork. The south terns joined the ruckus and, apparently just for the devil of it, dipped down to give the gull chick a peck on top of the head. With wild screams, the enraged gulls chased the terns off.

Gil and I took our leave in a hurry. Looking back from a distance, we saw the parent gulls sitting side by side,

WANDERING TATTLER WATCHING OVER ITS YOUNG NEAR CAMP
The bird appropriated the territory for her unconcerned, busy, downy young

as if consoling one another over the weight of their re-
sponsibility. We called this their "togetherness pose."

At the south end of the lake, we clambered down over
the rim on large boulders. A quarter mile below, we
reached the springs at the head of Loon Creek, which
we followed south until the stream increased in volume.

Gil peered into the water. "Looks good. I see fish.
Let's go farther downstream until we find a good fishing
hole."

Protected from the north wind, we were much warmer
here. Grass grew lush and tall. Willows, thick around
the stream, blocked our view. Were any bears lurking
about? We kept a sharp lookout.

We hiked through bi-colored Lupine (*Lupinus arcticus*) and gorgeous rosy Fireweed (*Epilobium augusti-
folium*). In a sheltered cove at about 1,600-feet elevation, there was an isolated cluster of a dozen Cottonwood
trees (*Populus tacamahaca*). Sturdy and mature, the lar-

A DOWNY GULL CHICK SWAM FAR OUT ON THE LAKE
The waves rocked him up and down like a cork

COTTON SEDGE, *ERIOPHORUM SCHEUCHZERI*, GREW AT THE
EDGE OF THE LAKE

Cassiope tetragona. Heather carpeted some of the high slopes.

Rhododendron lapponicum. Arctic Rhododendron, a shin-high shrub, grew in sheltered moist tundra.

A Rock Lichen. Rocks on the high ridges were unbelievably beautiful, like gorgeous abstract paintings.

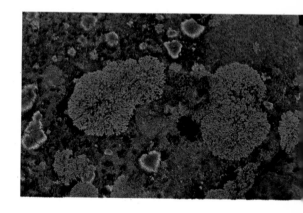

Vaccinium vitis-idaea. Ground Cranberries, called Lingenberries by Scandinavians, are delicious served with meat.

Band of Caribou crossing a high snowy pass in June, Brooks Range

MEW GULLS IN A "TOGETHERNESS" POSE
Male on the right

gest, as thick as a man's thigh, was a "bear tree"—a grizzly scratching post! The rugged bark of the poplar was badly scarred and mutilated. The beasts had chewed and clawed their signatures on this signpost. Strands of yellowish grizzly hair were caught in the craggy bark.

A "bear tree" serves as a sort of post office for the burly brutes. Each passing grizzly can measure his height and strength. He can get messages of who of his species has passed by recently—and who is the roughest and toughest character of the hills. We got their message. Some were rough and tough, all right.

Gil finally found a pool large enough to suit his fancy and began assembling his fishing gear.

"You'll have to stand guard." He handed me Big Bertha. "Keep your back to me and face the other direction. I'll try to keep one eye on the opposite bank."

We stood back-to-back and Gil began casting. It was

COTTONWOODS *(POPULUS TACAMAHACA)* SOUTH OF LOON LAKE
An isolated cluster of trees in a protected cove

GIL LEANING ON "BEAR TREE" SOUTH OF LOON LAKE

"BEAR TREE" SOUTH OF LOON LAKE
Here each passing grizzly could get messages of who, of his species, had gone by recently—and who was the roughest character of the hills.

spooky in that thick clump of willows with twelve-foot Feltleafs obstructing the view on both sides of the creek.

Gil had a strike! Soon he was a happy man, totally absorbed with fishing. He hauled in four Arctic Char, ten inches long. There must be more fish in the hole. He cast again.

Forgetting about grizzly-watching, I discovered a spring-fed green pool a few yards away. I was held spellbound by the matchless beauty of green velvety moss floating on the water, with stately shafts of brilliant red Sourdock (*Rumex arcticus*) accentuating the edges. Delicate blue Jacob's Ladder (*Polemonium acutiflorum*) bloomed in profusion. I gazed as if hypnotized at exquisite chartreuse strands of algae, like mermaid's tresses, swaying in the gentle current.

"If one of us gets mauled by a grizzly, there'll be no

doctor," Gil said crossly. "You'd better pay attention. This is dangerous business."

I vowed not to be distracted again.

We fought our way through rough grass and tangled waist-high shrubs for one more mile downstream to where the creek flowed slowly through a series of deep quiet pools. Gil had spotted these pools from the rim. What he found was beyond a fisherman's wildest expectations. We looked into the pools and saw them teeming with more fish than a hatchery. At the inlets, the larger fish hogged the choicest spots for feeding.

The shore was grassy and open, with good visibility. Grizzly-guarding was not so nerve-wracking.

My nimrod was soon pulling out 14- to 17-inch fat grayling and Arctic Char. Smaller fish were tossed back without regrets. One of the terns flew down to join Gil in fishing. After a minute or two of silent hovering, the dainty swallow-like bird dove into the water with scarce-

GIL FISHING LOON CREEK, BELOW LOON LAKE
He found a fisherman's dream

PRIZE FISH
Top: Grayling has a large dorsal fin
Bottom: Arctic char has beautiful orange spots

GIL WAS SOON PULLING OUT FOURTEEN- TO SEVENTEEN-INCH
FAT GRAYLING AND ARCTIC CHAR

ly a splash, then rose with a fingerling. We watched the
tern fly with effortless deep wingbeats the two miles back
to the lake. It disappeared over the rim. Moments later,
it was winging toward us again to repeat its graceful
performance.

We envied the tern's ability to cover the distance in
moments with the ease and grace of a ballet dancer,
while we had to bumble along like a couple of moose,
struggling through the bushes over the rough terrain.

A hush came over the tundra that midnight as I stood
guard. Soft gray clouds floated lazily over the peaks.
The Arctic Tern hovered buoyantly—poetry in motion.
The man silently fished. There was only a faint "sst"
from the flashing line, the softest "plip" when the hook
hit the water. Then a Gray-cheeked Thrush's poignant
"Whit-whit cheer!" came from the willows a stone's
throw away, sad sweet notes played on two violin strings.

The dusky Arctic night held us in its spell. Our hearts
were full.

Chapter VIII

Arctic Midnight

> *We go out daily and nightly to feed the eyes on the horizon.*

ONE EVENING WE DECIDED TO CLIMB URSUS PEAK. AFTER studying the mountain from the opposite side of the valley, we had determined a route. With loaded summit packs and Gil carrying Big Bertha, we skirted Tern Peninsula, crossing a field of sunny yellow Arctic Poppies *(Papaver radicatum)* swaying in the breeze. Bright pink Shooting Stars *(Dodecatheon frigidum)* stood delicately beneath shin-high willows.

We soon reached the base of a firm solid ridge with dry short vegetation that was a pure joy to ascend. As we gained elevation, the ridge became precipitous and rocky, but the view was enchanting. Golden velvety moss, lacey Reindeer Moss lichens, with pink, blue and yellow flowers,* grew between the rocks. Oversize bumblebees dressed in black and yellow velvet were working on the flowers, which could hardly support the weight of their plump pollinators.

On a small lichen-covered shelf, we stopped to rest and glass for bears with our binoculars. No grizzlies in sight. Far below were the areas where we had hiked. We had an eagle's-eye view of the triangular delta island with

---

*Pink Plumes *(Polygonum bistorta)*, blue Monk's Hood *(Aconitum delphinipholium)* and yellow Spider Plant *(Saxifraga flagellaris)*.

tiny tent and shelter, our summer home. We gained a new perspective of the hourglass lake and the whole narrow valley. For the first time, we could see the sharp pinnacle of Loon Peak* across the valley to the west. The sun was just behind it. Everywhere there was a fresh greenness. Summer had arrived.

Many sheep trails led around the rocks on the ridge. We continued climbing, scrambling around the cliffs, finding chimneys to scale. We were experiencing that certain childlike exhilaration that accompanies climbing on good solid rock.

"Oh, no!" I wailed. "My glasses. My prescription colored glasses. I left them below on the ledge." I turned and started to descend.

"Don't take time to go back now," Gil advised. "We'll

*Although Ursus Peak has now been officially named, Loon Peak is the only peak in the vicinity that was named on our topographic map.

FAR BELOW WERE AREAS WHERE WE HAD HIKED
We saw our delta island "home" gaining new perspective. Tern Peninsula is in the center.

get them on the way down. Do you remember where you left them?"

"Of course. I remember distinctly the rock I was sitting on. I know exactly where I laid them when I removed them to use my binoculars."

"Okay. So you have nothing to worry about. We'll pick them up on the way back."

We resumed the climb. The ridge narrowed and grew steeper. Happily we scrambled skyward on large lichen-covered blocks.

Gil led up a twelve-foot chimney. I followed until something bumped the top of my head. Gil was backing down again.

"That route looked good. Why didn't you go on through?"

"Well," he replied sheepishly, "near the top a spider had worked to make a perfect web across the chimney. I didn't have the stomach to wreck it. We'll find another way."

Most of the metamorphosed rocks on the ridge were gray. A few were white quartzite. Many were decorated in beautiful abstract designs of many colors. We wondered why the most colorful rock lichens were at the 3,000- to 3,500-foot elevations. Higher up the black rock lichens take over.

The ridge went up and up, then leveled off slightly, until we could see most of the remaining route to the summit. Since we had clear views on either side of the narrow ridge, Gil decided it would be safe to leave the rifle and pick it up on the way back.

The ridge was longer than we thought. We were in the land of those sky-dwellers, the Dall Sheep. Here on the desolate wind-swept ridges were their smoothed and leveled "beds," with bits of white wool and pellets scattered about. When icy winter blasts raked the crest, they sought protection on the lee side.

At 4,300-feet elevation, a pair of tiny Baird's Sandpipers appeared on the ridge above. They tried desperately to intercept us, to lead us in another direction with their pathetic broken-wing postures. What a bleak habitat for downy baby birds.

The last hundred feet to the summit were scaled with insecure footing on steep loose sliding rock.

"That was pretty tricky. Should have been roped, you know," I remarked with hindsight.

At the top we realized we had climbed the most difficult wall. A few hundred yards to our right there was an easier way.

It was midnight, but light enough to read our topographic map while we ate lunch on the Dall's sky-scraping summit. The nocturnal sun was a fiery red disk on

AT AN ELEVATION OF 4,300 FEET, THIS TINY BAIRD'S
SANDPIPER APPEARED ON THE RIDGE
The birds tried desperately to lead us in another direction

the northern horizon. The dazzling orb, amidst gilt-edged billowing clouds, refused to set. It bounced along from peak to peak, a majestic living ball of fire traveling east. Sky and mountains were suffused in bright alpenglow.

Gil and I were transported by the technicolor spectacular. It was unreal, euphoric. We seemed detached from the earth, suspended on waves of mystical music over a world of peace, quiet and beauty. Civilization was far away, and we seemed no longer to belong to that strange species that lived there with its pressures and neuroses.

The impact of our solitude was enormous. As though in a fantastically exquisite cathedral, we gazed over hauntingly beautiful wild peaks stretching endlessly in all directions. Only the wild creatures shared this tremendous untamed land with us, land that belonged to *them.* We were filled with a deep tranquility.

ON HIGH, WINDSWEPT RIDGES, WHAT A BLEAK
HABITAT FOR NESTING

Although we were in no hurry to leave our mountain-top concert hall, we made a rapid descent. Below steep crumbly cliffs, near the sandpipers, we stopped for long draughts of cool pure water from a tiny bubbling brook. After picking up the rifle, we took time to sit and gaze again at the valley below, where the sun shone obliquely on the slopes. Then, in search of my eyeglasses, I led the way to where I was certain they were. We looked for hours, traversing back and forth on the steep slope, but could find neither the rock nor the ledge I had remembered so vividly.

The mid-morning sun was shining brightly on the tent when we limped into camp with feet blistered from "side-hill gouging" as we looked for the glasses. We fixed a quick hot meal and went to bed.

※   ※   ※

Time went quickly for us in the wilderness. There was always much work to be done—nests to check, plants and specimens to collect and care for, places to explore. Days were never dull. We were completely happy, even during physical discomforts, and we derived satisfaction from being capable of taking care of ourselves, of turning problems into challenges to be overcome.

Nearly every day, we wandered out from camp, roaming over the mountain slopes, prowling through the valleys. One misty morning, we were heading south for another fishing trip below the lake.

"Let's cut across that bend, hit the creek a mile below the good fishing hole, and work back up," Gil suggested.

Two hours later, we were striding on a golden velour carpet under Feltleaf Willows on the banks of Lower Loon Creek. Gil was leading the way with fishing and

VIVIAN, WITH ICE AXE, GOING DOWN A MOUNTAIN,
HIKING THROUGH DWARF BIRCH
Nearly every day we wandered out from camp, roaming over the slopes

ALASKA NEST RECORD CARD
University of Alaska, College, Alaska

Name and address of observer: Mr. & Mrs. Gilbert Steander, 13900 Southwest Sundeleaf Dr., Lake Oswego, Oregon 97034

FOR OBSERVATIONS ON ONE NEST

Day	Month	No. of Eggs	No. of Young	Adult on Nest? Sex?	Time
27	6	1	4	♀	
1	7	1	4		
1	7	collected egg			
9	7	Fledged			

REMARKS: e.g. Birds banded, pertinent weather information, etc.

Sample # 11

Name of Bird: Tree Sparrow   Year: 1964
Locality of Nest: Loon Lake
Latitude 67°55' N Longitude 157°20' W
Altitude 2350' Direction slope faces West

Nest ....on.... ft. above ground or base of cliff

TYPE OF VEGETATION IN AREA (check one or more)
Forest ☐   Tall brush (4-10') ☐   Shrub (1-4') ☐
Moist Tundra ☒   Rocky Tundra ☐   Field ☐   Marsh ☐

Other ....

List abundant plants:
(Cottongrass)
Eriophorum vaginatum

POSITION OF NEST
In tree, brush or shrub ☐
On ground, under tree, brush or shrub ☐
On ground, not under tree, brush or shrub ☒
On ground, in open on sand or rocks ☐
On cliff or bank ☐   On floating mat ☐
On building ☐

FATE OF NEST
No. of eggs hatched ....4....
No. of unhatched eggs ....1....
Cause of non-hatching of eggs ..sterile..
....
No. of chicks that left nest ....4....
Cause of death of chicks not leaving nest:........................

THERE WAS ALWAYS MUCH WORK TO BE DONE
Nests to check, records to keep

VIVIAN COLLECTING PLANTS
Pyrola grandiflora and *Astragalus umbellatus*

VIV PRESSING PEAVINES *(ASTRAGALUS UMBELLATUS)*
Fragrant shield fern *(Dryopteris fragrans)* in right hand

camera equipment, while I was saddled with Big Bertha.

"Look. It's a cabin!" Gil emerged from the willows. "Well, it *almost* was a cabin."

Weathered spruce logs lay criss-crossed, outlining where a cabin had been started many years ago.

"This was never finished. No roof was ever put on. Must have been Eskimo, because it's so low." Gil studied the ruins. "The logs had to be brought up from treeline in winter by dog sled. Probably planned to cover it with sod—a sod igloo."

But these ruins were being used. Not by Eskimos, but by grizzlies. It was another grizzly scratching station. The beasts had marched around and around the crumbling structure until their pads had worn a telltale trail. Tufts of tawny grizzly hair were caught on the corner logs.

Beyond the ruins, Gil found a deep quiet pool where

TIME WENT QUICKLY FOR US IN THE WILDERNESS
We had specimens to collect and care for. *From fingertips:* Harlequin, gray-cheeked thrush, tree-sparrow eggs.

A teetering Spotted Sandpiper resented our intrusion

Arctostaphylos Alpina. Bearberry. The fruit provided a feast for the birds and small mammals.

Polemonium b o r e a l e . This northern Jacob's Ladder has a delicate yellow throat.

Dryas octopetala. We were happy to see this familiar species that also grows on the high slopes of Mount Hood.

Claytonia sarmentosa. Spring Beauty. Shy and delicate, they wore their pink veined petals like ballerina skirts.

VIV PICKED GRIZZLY HAIR FROM A SOD IGLOO RUINS WHICH
HAD BEEN USED FOR A SCRATCHING STATION

We think these ruins, down toward timberline, were the remains of a hut
begun by an Eskimo and never finished. The roof would have been very
low—typical Eskimo style—and the entire structure covered with sod.

the creek wound under a cliff. Large grayling swam lazily in the aquamarine depths. Gil began fishing.

I climbed up a curious 100-foot-high round hill which stood prominently nearby and discovered it was a giant frost-heave, a "pingo," with fresh wet clay exuding from the top, much like molten lava from a volcano. The mud flow extended over the south side. These pingos are formed when the top surface pushes down on the permafrost below, and then freezes. Resulting pressures force the still-fluid clays through cracks to the surface.

Gil joined me on top of the pingo, where we sat watching some Say's Phoebes feeding young in a crevice of the cliff above Gil's newfound fishing hole. An Arctic Ground Squirrel came skipping up the hill. Standing up tall on his hind legs, he viewed us with suspicion. We held still. The Parka Squirrel chirped his displeasure

VIV CARRYING "BIG BERTHA"

These logs are at the site where an Eskimo started a hut but never finished it. Roof and doorway would have been very low, with the entire structure covered with sod—a sod igloo.

at our invasion of his privacy, emphasizing it with a quick flip of his tail, then ducked into his burrow.

A Long-tailed Jaeger, hovered in graceful elegance over the flats across the creek near a young bull moose feeding in a pond. Bulking large and dark over the low vegetation, the moose splashed out onto the cottongrass and sedately made his way toward treeline.

Climbing back up to the rim of Loon Lake, Gil and I came upon two porcupines fraternizing. Wearing their long yellow hair combed back at a rakish angle, they ambled along together between the boulders. When Gil approached for a picture, one turned and hid his head in a crevice between the rocks, like a bashful child. This exposed his white stickery pants. When Gil whistled softly, the porky could not resist turning around for an inquisitive look.

On the morning of July 10th, donning our caps and jackets as protective coverning, we went over to Tern

THE PINGO, A GIANT FROST HEAVE
Fresh wet clay, exuded from the top, is flowing down the opposite side

YOUNG BULL MOOSE

A YOUNG BULL MOOSE FEEDING IN A POND

Peninsula to make a neighborly call. Small Snow Willow leaves had emerged. Some anemones *(Anemone narcissiflora)* and a few sprigs of sparse grass had sprung up, adding traces of greenery to the drab monotones of the dry tundra. We found that the terns' eggs had hatched. Though agitated parents lashed us with fury, we insisted on seeing their new babies. When we could not find them, I backed off, to ease their worry. Gil stood near the empty nest, not daring to step for fear of crushing a camouflaged chick. He was right, for he finally spotted a small bit of streaked gray fluff with pinkish feet and bill just inches from his boot. The newborn huddled motionless, hiding his head under an anemone leaf. We didn't try to locate the nestmate.

The water level of the lake was rising very slowly but steadily as frost melted out of the tundra. The bare rocks all around the shore indicated that the water did rise

PORKY

He wore his long yellow hair combed back at a rakish angle

PORCUPINE

He lived at the south end of Loon Lake and he had stickery pants

OUR WATER GAUGE

At the lower right. The water level rose nearly to the top of the stick during the flood. South arm of Aquila on the left, Lover's Gully in the middle background.

occasionally to the overflow level, probably during a heavy rainfall. If this happened, our camp would be flooded. To be on the safe side, we contrived a way to measure just how far the water was rising. Just above the water level, we made a large rock cairn to hold a vertical willow pole, with bark girdled every foot. From camp we could easily read our "water gauge" with binoculars.

Chapter IX

Tussocks, Tension, Treeline

> *. . . on the bare ground . . . all mean egotism vanishes.*

GIL AND I HAD A LONGING FOR REAL TREES. WE MISSED THE green conifers of Oregon and wistfully gazed at the spruces we could see from the south rim of Loon Lake, estimating them to be ten or twelve miles away. Thus, the middle of July found us preparing for a four-day journey. But before leaving the area, we took a quick trip up to check the eggs in the Rough-legs' aerie. High above the nest, we looked down on three balls of white cotton sprawled on the spacious platform. The anxious parent hawks hovered over us until we departed, mission accomplished. We knew how many had hatched.

Back at camp, our packs were loaded with the two-man back-packing tent, sleeping bag, food, cookpots and camera equipment. Leaving our camp unattended for several days was a gamble, but we had no other choice if we were to explore the Arctic tree limit. With the collection of pesticide samples hung in the Klepper, we zipped it up securely, hoping no wild animals would scent and destroy the specimens. The front of the shelter was closed off with a tarp. I carried my diary and the record books, in case the camp should be raided. Gil carried Big Bertha.

The robins on the islet near camp now had three lusty

youngsters. With farewell glances at our other bird neighbors, busy with their young, we waded the stream and set out eagerly for another adventure.

Since our only mode of travel in the Arctic was by shank's mare, our legs had become strong. We were in top physical condition, without a care in the world. Making our way around the east side of the lake, we stopped at the gulls' peninsula to see how they were faring. Parents were not aggressive. We didn't see any chick.

"Let's go," I urged. "We have a long trip before us."

Gil glanced ahead to the shoulder of the mountain, where our route lay. I was already on my way, dropping into a gully we had to cross.

"That's funny," Gil chuckled. "That rock up there against the sky looks just like a big old wolf sitting on his haunches." He leaned over to pick up his pack, then did a double take.

"JUST A DARN MINUTE!"
Gil did a double take. "Did I see that rock move?"

"Just a darn minute! Did I see that rock move?" Instead of his pack, Gil picked up his binoculars.

"By golly! That's a grizzly!"

I lost no time in scrambling back up to Gil.

"He's scratching himself. Sitting up like a fat old dog, looking all around."

"Lucky you saw him when you did." I watched the fearsome beast through my binoculars.

"Yeah. From this point on he would've been out of our line of vision until we were right below him."

"Wow! What do we do now?" I put down my pack.

"We have three choices. To go left of the grizzly, we will have to backtrack and climb up a thousand feet— but we might meet him up there. We can sneak below him, along the shore, under the bank—but we could meet him eyeball to eyeball there too. Or we can turn around and go back to camp."

We stood on the peninsula, debating which course to take. The bear still sat there scratching. The wind was in our favor. I glanced behind us, to see if there were any grizzlies in that direction.

"What route do you choose?" Gil asked.

"I hate to go back to camp after all the preparation. I'll vote the low route—by the lake." We would have a long detour either way, but I thought Gil could handle any situation, since he had the rifle.

"I don't like that way. It's too close to the bear, and we couldn't keep an eye on him. He could be right on top of us before we'd see him. I'd rather go the high road."

"Just think of all the work to climb way up there with these heavy packs. Let's go by the shore. It is closer to the bear—and scarier, but we would have it over with quicker. What do you say?"

"That's awfully close quarters." Gil mopped his brow. "If we meet him, I'll have time for only one shot. What if I miss? Well, okay. Let's get it over with."

The grizzly was in the same position when we dropped down to tread on the rocks along the waterline. A ten-foot embankment obstructed our view of the bear, and there were several hundred yards to go before we could check again on the beast's whereabouts. From our observations of *Ursus horribilis*, we were certain of only one thing—grizzlies are completely unpredictable. The bear could start galloping our way at any moment or go another way—or flop down and go to sleep.

The gulls suddenly swooped down on us as their little one swam out from the shore ahead of us and paddled swiftly out on the lake. Screaming their anger, the parents narrowly missed our heads. The south terns joined the melee. A large loon was out on the lake, calmly watching the commotion.

"As if we didn't have enough to worry about. I hope they don't attract the bear's attention."

Trying to ignore the attacking terns and gulls, Gil led the way warily along the shore, holding the rifle with both hands, ready to fire. I followed close behind.

"Don't crowd so close to me," Gil complained. "What if I'd have to turn around quick?"

I watched the bank on our left, wishing fervently the birds would let us alone.

"You know," Gil muttered, "that bear could be right above us at this moment. I wish we had gone the other way. At least we would know what the bear was doing."

"Just hurry," I urged impatiently. "Let's have it done with."

But Gil would not hurry. A blind spot ahead worried him. We were clambering over large boulders lying in the water, sometimes having to jump to the next one.

Seeing that their precious darling had made it safely away from us, the gulls followed him solicitously. Then the terns seemed to lose interest in us.

"That pilot said he saw a grizzly lie in wait on a bank and pounce on a caribou crossing below it," I suddenly remembered. I fancied the bear waiting for us around the next corner.

"I wish I knew where he is. I'd rather be out in the open, even closer to him, if I only knew what to expect." Gil jumped to another boulder.

The tension-packed minutes passed slowly. At long last we reached a point where we had some space between us and the bank. Finally, we could see the grizzly —feeding, still in the same place.

Skirting the end of the lake, still too close to the grizzly, we circled far to the right, gaining a respectful distance between us and the unpredictable wild one, who suddenly began moving up the valley toward our camp.

"Maybe it will demolish our camp." I pictured the chaos.

"Shall we go back to protect it?" Gil offered.

Again we stood debating which course to take.

"Let's take the gamble." I was becoming fatalistic. "We'll find out when we get back. Okay?"

"Okay with me."

Caribou trails traversing the base of the mountain made easy traveling. The packs were heavy, but we didn't mind. At last we were really on our way and the going looked good. The spruces, far in the distance, beckoned.

A family of four ravens accompanied us, entertaining with clownish aerial acrobatics and odd-sounding croaks and cronks. Some of their talk was bell-like in quality.

The wide U-shaped valley stretched on, with gentle contours like a rolling golf course. The green vegetation looked smooth. Entering a field of cottongrass tussocks, we began treading our way through, stepping between the tufts on firm gravelly soil.

"Cottongrass isn't so bad to travel through," Gil stated cheerfully, forgetting our last experience with it. "We're making good time. I don't think it's as terrible as it's cracked up to be."

A snipe flushed, flew a zig-zag course and went down into the grass again.

Not long after this, we felt our boots sink deep into wet clay between the tussocks. About a pound of mud was lifted with each step. How could the soil be so wet and sticky on the side of a hill? The grass tussocks grew higher and closer together where the soil was wet. It was so laborious to lift our legs high enough to clear the clumps, that we tried using them for stepping blocks to keep us out of the ooze they grew in. With heavy packs, keeping our balance was tricky. Walking on the tops worked well—for about three steps, then a wobbly one would throw us off balance. I sprawled across one of them, my knees in the muck.

"Oh, crum! I've had enough of this."

We looked around in desperation. Which way to go? We were in a sea of this grassy abomination.

"A mile farther on is that dry looking tundra. Let's head for that."

Struggling on, we promised ourselves not to be trapped again by that innocent golf course appearance.

"Hey. I've just had a bright idea!" I announced. "We have to lift our legs high enough to clear the darn clumps anyway, so let's make the most of it. Take as long steps as possible. Maybe even clear two at once!" I changed pace, leaping.

"Are you kidding?" Gil watched incredulously.

A few such leaps and I'd had it.

"Silly idea, wasn't it?" I admitted sheepishly.

Once again we tried the balancing act of stepping on the tops of the clumps. If two clumps were close enough together, we had one good solid step, but these did not occur often. It was slow and exhausting work over the longest mile and a half we had ever hiked. Even worse than the cottongrass were the few shallow gullies with shoulder-high tangles of alder thickets. "Alder-bashing," we fought our way through blindly, dreading the thought of stumbling onto a grizzly.

At last, by angling up slightly, we reached a rounded ridge of blessed dry tundra. We were learning from hard experience what terrains made the best traveling. From now on, we would seek out the lighter-colored, drier, shorter vegetation that grew on firm soil.

We descended into a rocky ravine and sat on smooth slabs of rock to drink from the cool, clear stream. It was a delightful place to rest and eat. We ravenously devoured some of Gil's incomparable homemade bread and rolls—with sausage.

Back out of the ravine, we continued traversing the southern arm of Ursus. Down in the valley, Loon Creek meandered southeast, with a thousand oxbow bends cutting through the abominable cottongrass. A number of

THE EXASPERATING COTTON GRASS TUSSOCKS MADE
TEDIOUS TRAVELING

oval lakes across the creek, glistened mirror-like in the
sun. With rising excitement, we drank in the closer view
of our destination. Dark green spires, spruce trees,
crowded around Loon and Agiak creeks where they join
to form Hunt Fork River. An enormous white field of
overflow ice, a mile or so long, lay on the wide river bed,
framed by the trees.

Happily, we began a gradually descending traverse,
heading for the conifers. We had about five more miles
to go.

Suddenly, Gil stopped and sat down.

"We've got to stop. I can't go on."

"What is it?" I asked.

"Sharp pains! Here." He pointed to his abdomen, near
his right groin. "I feel like vomiting."

Gil was a very sick man, I could see that. A picture
of abject misery. Slipping his arms out of his packstraps,

he let his pack fall to the ground. I had taken the rifle from him.

"I'll be all right if I rest a while," he insisted. Then he stretched out on the ground. Fortunately, we were out of the cottongrass. This was smooth dry tundra.

Now it was up to me to keep grizzly-watch. I wondered where the last one had gone. With binoculars, I glassed all around. Any dun-colored hump could be a sleeping grizzly. None of them moved.

I took off my pack and sat down beside my sick husband.

"What do you think it is?" I asked anxiously.

"Gas pressure, probably. It will go away if I rest."

But the pains persisted. Gil groaned and turned over on his face. I checked some grizzly-colored humps. This would be a bad time to spot a grizzly.

"What if it is appendicitis?" I thought to myself. That is one problem we would not be able to cope with. We were strong and healthy, but that could lay low the strongest. It was frightening to see my usually rugged and healthy husband writhing in pain. He tried to vomit. I had never felt so helpless.

After a while, Gil started to get up.

"Are you feeling better?"

"No, but we can't stay here. Maybe if I stand up and walk, the pain will go away."

But he was unable to travel. He lay face down again and retched.

"I'll be all right. Don't worry."

But I was worried. Terribly so. A feeling of desperation came over me. What action should I take? It was up to me. No one could decide for me. *I had to do it alone.*

Hoary Marmot, relative of the woodchuck, lives as far north as the Arctic Coast.
He hibernates in winter.

Salix. Snow Willow lay prostrate on the ground. All woody branches lay on or under the surface, protected from severe winds.

Vaccinum uliginosum. Luscious Blueberries were relished by all of us. Delicious, served with Dream Whip.

Eriophorum vaginatum. Cottongrass. We vowed not to be trapped again by that innocent golf-course appearance.

Geum glaciale. Glacier Avens and Bumblebee. Flowers could hardly support the weight of their plump pollinators.

My anxieties intensified as I looked around us at the vast expanse of wilderness. It looked so vacant and wild —and impersonal. Like a drowning man clutching for a straw, I searched the empty skies for a plane. The impact of our isolation hit me like a thunderbolt. I knew, as surely as I was sitting there, that if the pains persisted, we were in real trouble. Before Andy Anderson, our bushpilot, had left us in the wilderness, I had asked him if there was some way to contact him in case of emergency. Of course, the answer was no.

My mind raced frantically over the many possibilities. If Gil's illness continued, I would have to leave him lying helpless and alone on the tundra while I rushed back to camp for our supply of penicillin, brought for just such an emergency. Could I get it in time? Even if I did, the drug would be only a temporary help.

We had only one rifle for protection. I would have to leave it with him, because some wild predator may assault a defenseless creature lying sick or injured on the ground.

Alone, with no firearms, I would be terribly afraid of encountering grizzlies. How would I react if I met one? Would I panic and run?

"You never know how much strength or courage you have in reserve until you need it," my mother had once told me. "Then a higher Power will give you what you need." Her remarkable courage and good humor through great physical suffering was a living testimony of that truism.

I prayed. I watched for grizzlies. I lost track of time.

At last my mind was made up. I got up, to start the run back to camp.

Gil stirred. Sensing what was in my mind, he stood

up and tried to walk. Impossible. He had to lie down again.

It was a shock to see him so ill. *I could not make myself leave him,* so I waited. Again I sat numbly losing track of time.

Gil threw up, and I thought again of appendicitis and its symptoms. "I believe I'm a little better," he spoke, weakly.

My hopes rose. I waited patiently, glad I had not left him.

"The pain is easing," Gil sat up, grimacing.

"You look sort of green around the gills."

"That's the way I feel. But I want to try to go on in a little while."

I took a few things out of his pack to lighten his load, but my small frame could not carry much more weight than it already had. Having to be the strong one was a new and sudden experience for me.

"Okay, let's try it." He got up and I helped him with his pack. He looked wobbly. There was still some pain.

For the first mile or so, progress was painfully slow. Although the terrain made fair traveling, we stopped often to rest. Gradually, however, over those last interminable miles to the spruce trees, Gil began to feel better. My spirits were soaring on waves of relief as we approached the first tree. I patted it fondly.

Chapter X

Hunt Fork, Northern Tree Limit

*The tempered light of the woods is
like a perpetual morning, and is stim-
ulating.*

ALL OF A SUDDEN, WE WERE WALKING IN A DELIGHTFUL
forest, on springy Reindeer Moss carpeting. The straight
brown boles of White Spruce (*Picea glauca*), named for
its white wood, were magnificent. The pointed crowns
stood forty or fifty feet tall. Slender sentinels of the
northern forest, these conifers have very short branches,
unlike the firs we knew in Oregon.

We spotted a Varied Thrush, that elusive woods sprite
whose poignant quavering calls haunt the forest with
"Find meeeee—find meeeee," then ventriloquially, as
echoing from a sepulchre, "Here——I am——."

Ruby-crowned Kinglets, tiny atoms of birds, lisped
and scolded in the trees. A family of Gray Jays wandered
by.

"Look at that!" Gil exclaimed. "A double-decker robin
nest! There's a triple-decker—and even four!" They were
on the lower branches of the conifers, near the trunk.
These robins like their nest sites so much that they keep
building on the same spot year after year after year.
Dense, flat-needle branches formed sloping roofs over
the nest, not only shedding rain, but screening out predators.

THE LAST SPRUCES OF THE NORTHERN TREE LIMIT,
ABOVE HUNT FORK

NORTHERN TREE LIMIT, HUNT FORK
Note the "overflow" ice on the river at right of center

A FEW LARGE, OBNOXIOUS FLIES BUZZED AROUND
One bit me. A botfly? Revolted, I swatted it

"Can that be a shorebird?" I asked. "Sounds like zylophone notes going down the scale."

We stopped to look all around us in the knee-high grass.

"Let's go on. I need to rest," Gil informed me. "I'm anxious to find a campsite."

We had no more than started when Gil stopped.

"Hey. I see it. On the top of that spruce."

A large tan shorebird, gracefully holding out its wings, balanced on the swaying tip in a delicate treetop ballet. It was providing its own music.

"An Upland Plover. How wonderful to find these birds here in the wilderness. After the way they were treated by man and nearly exterminated, like the Passenger Pigeon, I don't blame them for getting far from civilization."

The Upland Plover followed from treetop to treetop,

calling its zylophone notes, as we moved through the spruces. We found an exquisite little spot beside a small gurgling stream, a couple hundred yards above the Hunt Fork River—the end of our journey. Our pedometer showed we had come more than ten miles from base camp at Loon Lake.

Heaving great sighs of relief, we shrugged off our heavy packs and sank down on a luxurious cushion of thick springy green moss. An inquisitive Red Squirrel peered out of dense lower branches of a spruce close to us. He didn't scold. He only stared, without fear, having never seen anything like us before. We were charmed by the engaging creature.

Upland Plovers were still calling from the spruce tips. In the distance, a Flicker's voice, "Yucka—yucka—yucka!"

We were enchanted by the forest and its inhabitants. "In the woods is perpetual youth . . . a decorum and

AN UPLAND PLOVER
I don't blame them for getting far from civilization after the way they were treated by man and nearly exterminated, as was the passenger pigeon.

sanctity reign . . . every hour and season yields its trib-
utes of delight."

The change from the wide open spaces of the tundra,
with its low vegetation, was refreshing, and we realized
how much we had missed trees, so green and beautiful.
And so much more friendly than Feltleaf Willows. Or
so it seemed—perhaps because the squirrels in the spruces
are less fearsome than grizzlies in Feltleaf thickets.

"If we're going to have fried fish for supper, we'd better
get down to the river." Gil had recuperated.

"Like walking on pillows," I exulted, as we tripped
downhill on the spongy mosses. Without our packs, we
were walking on air.

Down on the gravel bars, a teetering Spotted Sandpiper resented our intrusion vociferously. Tracks in the
mud told us that a moose and a small canine, either fox
or young wolf, had been there before us.

"There are porcupine tracks and these look like River
Otter." Gil studied the footprints in the sand.

He selected a promising-looking pool and began fishing while I stood guard with Big Bertha. Gil nudged me
and pointed to a golden-haired porcupine sitting on its
haunches on the opposite side of the pool. It was quietly
eating River Beauty (*Epilobium latifolium*), using its
hands to cram the lovely flowers into his mouth.

"The porky sees us. I'm glad he's not afraid. Isn't he
charming? Look at his velvety nose," I purred softly.
I didn't want to break the spell.

Narrow channels of the river wound through wide
gravel bars. Spruces, cottonwoods and willows crowded
the banks, obstructing our view beyond the river bed.

I watched Gil's fishhook hit the water. Eyeing us, the
porcupine munched the purple fireweed.

This was the witching hour, approaching midnight, when mammals like to be moving about. I turned around, straining my ears, holding my breath. How quiet. There was a hush, as if all creatures had paused to listen too.

It didn't take long for Gil to catch seven grayling. Puffing back up the hill to our campsite, we were weary and remembered the hard miles we had come. Mosquitoes swarmed around us. Their high-pitched humming was annoying, but after we used insect repellent on our hands and faces, they left us alone.

It was eerie as we lay down with the rifle beside us, in a secret place under unfamiliar trees. No one else in the whole world knew where we were. We slept like babies on our soft bed of moss.

"What was that?" Gil sat up. A thunderous roar had awakened us. It still reverberated through the valley.

"Oh, I know what it was." He lay down again. "Ice breaking off the glacier."

CAMP IN THE SPRUCES AT HUNT FORK
It was eerie as we lay down, with the rifle beside us, in this secret place under the unfamiliar trees.

"I wonder what adventure today will bring." I sat up eagerly. "Let's get up and go exploring."

Berries were ripening. Around camp Crowberries (*Empetrum nigrum*) and Ptarmigan Berries (*Arctostaphylos rubra*) were turning color. Lupines, past blooming, were abundant. Tips of the spruces were pregnant with brown cones.

Exploring the narrow forest corridor, we met another Red Squirrel. This one was beside himself with agitation, his small frame convulsed with repeated expletives. He scolded. He ranted. He swore. We were denounced by every insult in his vocabulary—all, we observed with amazement, while he held a spruce cone in his mouth like a cigar. In the spruces, the irascible rodent had a number of bulky nests made of leaves and vegetable fibers. The ground beneath was riddled with his burrows.

Returning to the river bed, we wandered downstream. This was a "braided" stream. The winding channels intertwined, separating and joining repeatedly in the wide

TIPS OF THE SPRUCES WERE PREGNANT WITH BROWN CONES

WE WERE DENOUNCED BY EVERY INSULT IN THE BOOK
All this insolence was being dished out while he held a spruce cone in his
mouth like a cigar.

river bed. Crossing the channels was sometimes easy, but when too deep for our boots, I waded barefoot in the icy water. Gil removed his boots and socks but put his shoepacs back on to protect his tender feet. I paid the price of a painful crossing in order to have dry boots on the other side.

A dark gyrfalcon cried with annoyance when we disturbed him from his favorite perch on a cliff above the river.

A large field of overflow ice lay ahead. This was the glacier we had seen from the distance, when looking down on the treeline. We proceeded until a swift two-foot-deep stream separated us from the ice. Using poles to steady ourselves in the swift current, we reached the wall of ice. It was overhanging and over six feet high. Standing barefoot in the ice water, I could not get up on

HIKING THE GRAVEL BARS, HUNT FORK RIVER
Ice overhang (*upper right*) from a great field of overflow ice eight to ten feet thick.

the slippery hard ice. My feet were bruised and aching from the rocks and cold water. Painfully, I waded upstream, struggling to keep my balance in the swirling water. At last I found a place where I could climb out of the freezing river onto the ice.

Gil followed me, crossing quickly in comparative comfort, wearing his shoepacs. I live and learn.

Once on the smooth hard ice sheet, we had easy walking. The glacier was one hundred yards wide and over a mile long. A pair of Rough-legged Hawks had their aerie high on a cliff. Their three black-eyed downy young hung over the edge of the stick nest, ogling us in wonderment. Six Violet-green Swallows darted back and forth over the river, adeptly skimming mosquitoes out of the air. They returned with loaded beaks to crevices under a massive stick nest. A pair of Say's Phoebes also nested there.

Reaching the south shore of the river, we climbed up a break in the cliffs. It was a steep wet shale gully, as slippery as if it had been greased. We had to use alders for handholds before we made any progress. At the top we started hiking south along the rim. With consternation, we found ourselves in the midst of another expansive field of cottongrass tussocks. Chagrined, we slipped and skittered back down "Greasy Gully," another lesson learned on the vicissitudes of Arctic foot travel.

As we hiked back toward camp, our boots sent long silvery ice crystals tinkling over the glacier. This was "candled ice," slivers formed by the thawing and refreezing of glacier ice.

Gil showed me caribou tracks on the river bars, identifying them by the rounded edges of the hoof prints. A moose hoof is pointed. We also saw wolf tracks which measured five and a quarter by four and a half inches.

ICE CRYSTALS OF "CANDLED" ICE ON MELTING
OVERFLOW ICE

"CANDLED ICE"
Shoepac in ice crystals, overflow ice, Hunt Fork. The crystals tinkled like broken glass.

The Yellow-shafted Flicker came to call on us at camp. We found its nest hole in a spruce stub. Nestlings, soon to leave the nest, looked out at us, two at a time. We sat down on a rotten log to watch the young woodpeckers and disturbed a colony of large ants inhabiting the log. Then we realized that we had seen no ants at the Loon Lake elevation—or anywhere beyond the spruces. *There were no ants on the tundra.* No wonder flickers were here, since their favorite diet is ants.

We walked around camp in our bare feet, just to feel the soothing soft moss with our toes.

Gil fried more grayling. We craved green vegetables, so I picked some lupine pods. We ate them but were to learn later of the risk we took!

Loafing around camp, we noticed two moose loom up big and black across the river near a small tundra lake. They were the largest creatures we had seen. A cow, with last year's bull calf, strode long-leggedly toward the

YELLOW-SHAFTED FLICKERS HAD A NEST IN A SPRUCE
STUB AT HUNT FORK
Nestlings, about ready to fledge, looked out at us

river. The cow led the way, slowly, haltingly, looking around suspiciously, as if watching for something below on the river bed. The calf followed at her heels, looking back frequently. The beasts entered the trees on the opposite bank near the river. There they bedded down, remarkably inconspicuous.

We got a lot of satisfaction just knowing the moose were there. They were company for us, even though they were a half mile away.

We climbed up the slope behind camp to look for Upland Plover nests. Around midnight, we reached a flat dry ridge just above treeline.

"Wheet-ooooeeeeeeeeeeeeeeeooo!" We had found the plovers' territories. The cry was weird, like a long drawn-out "wolf whistle." A plover flew around us, like a will-o'-the wisp. Now we saw it, now we didn't. Another was in low bushes, acting as if it had young. I went over there. It gave a pathetic little cry, dragged its wings for a ways, then flew to another spot.

GIL WAS EXPEDITION COOK

ABOVE TIMBERLINE, LOOKING FOR UPLAND PLOVER NESTS
We listened to their wild, ghostly calls

"Hee-hee-hee-hee!" the bird tittered. I followed. It led me farther away. Again it laughed at me.

Gil was following another plover, with the same results. The birds tittered and snickered as they hid in the grass. They sneaked around with their heads down, went through broken-wing acts, then flew around with fast shallow wing beats, calling all the while. We finally tired of their monkeyshines and sat down—just to watch.

The wide valley floor was emerald green below, with paler, greyer shades of green where the slopes swept up to the mountains. Small pink puffs of clouds hung over frosted peaks to the west. The immense scene looked unspeakably wild and lonely, emphasizing our remoteness—and our unimportance. For the moment, we were no more significant than other creatures inhabiting the valley.

Our eyes found the two moose lying obscurely beside

the river. A pair of gulls and a tern hunted over the lake across from us. We watched them wing their way toward Loon Lake. They were probably our neighbors.

There was a muted roar from the streams below, then a crash like thunder. A great chunk of ice had calved from the glacier. I thought I heard the yapping howl of a young wolf. Or was it wishful thinking?

In the wee hours, when we crept into our sack, the hulking dark forms of the moose still added to our contentment.

Chapter XI

A Day in Water

> *Nature is a discipline. She pardons no mistakes. Her yea is yea, and her nay nay.*

THE TIME CAME TO PREPARE FOR OUR TREK BACK TO LOON Lake. We folded our red tent and cleaned up our campsite in the spruces. Only a few smoky stones remained as evidence that we had invaded this unblemished wilderness.

Saddled down with heavy packs again, we started out in late afternoon for base camp at the higher elevation. Gil carried Big Bertha. We elected not to return by the same route we had used on our trip down, even though it was shorter. The recollections of cottongrass hummocks were still painful. It would be easier, we thought, to follow the serpentine stream, with its smooth gravel bars. We thought!

As we started hiking along the bluff overlooking the river, a family of Slate-colored Juncos (Snowbirds) flitted ahead of us, and there was a flicker. A couple of plovers followed along, calling musically from spruce tip to spruce tip, as if urging us to hurry and begone.

Past the last of the conifers, in open country again, we scrambled down to the gravel bars, where we anticipated good fast traveling. Weather was ideal, with an immacu-

WE ELECTED NOT TO RETURN BY THE SAME ROUTE WE
HAD USED ON THE TRIP DOWN
Gil near Loon Creek, before leaving the spruces of Hunt Fork

late blue sky. It was just cool enough for comfortable
hiking. We were eager to go.

A few hundred yards along, the gravel bar ended
abruptly on our side of the stream. Since there was one
continuing on the opposite side and the water was not
deep, we decided to wade across. With our top-heavy
packs, we had trouble maintaining our balance as we
gingerly treaded across on the highest rocks in the stream
bed. In spite of our efforts to keep our feet dry, the water splashed over our boot tops.

When we reached the other shore, we put down our
packs, sat down and removed our boots to empty them
of water and to wring out our socks. Gil's boots had
hooks, but mine had eyelets and took longer to lace and
unlace.

Gil had to help me shoulder my pack again and we

marched on optimistically. A few moments later we stopped to watch another porcupine preoccupied with eating fireweed flowers. When we proceeded to walk close by, the animal went on with its meal, watching us casually out of the corner of his eye.

A half mile from where we had waded across the stream, the gravel bar ended on our side of the stream. It continued on the opposite side. Again we waded across, again we had to let down our packs, empty our boots and wring out our socks, and again we had to re-lace our boots. Gil laced his quickly. I tried to keep up with him, but my laces had no tips and were frayed.

Near a low shale bluff, two pairs of Violet-green swallows twittered and hawked over the stream, then flew to crevices in the cliff. All along the route were White-crowns—the most predominant bird species. A pair of Spotted Sandpipers tried to lead us from our path, tee-tering and bobbing excitedly, dragging their wings, feigning injury. A rufous-nosed Arctic Ground Squirrel crouched just two feet in front of Gil. It froze for several minutes, then scooted off into a burrow.

"I hear a plane!" Gil looked around in the cloudless sky. I didn't hear it. Neither of us could see one.

Leaving the spruces far behind, we followed Loon Creek, winding tortuously through the cottongrass valley. The stream bed, thirty- or forty-feet wide, varied in depth, but often the treeless banks were little higher than our heads. Occasional higher bluffs broke the monotony. We hiked through bright thick fields of rosy River Beauty.

We continued to follow the gravel bars, first on one side of the stream, then on the other. Each time we crossed and recrossed the fast waters, we had to follow the same ritual—set packs down, remove boots, empty them, wring out socks, put them back on wet, lace up boots, shoulder packs. The routine became tedious. Our feet were getting sore from hiking in wet socks. And with each mile—and crossing—our packs seemed heavier. To save time, we started wading recklessly across. It was futile to try to keep water out of our boots.

"I hear a plane!" Gil turned again to search the empty skies. I still didn't hear one. Considering how ex-pugilists hear non-existent bells ringing, I began to wonder if Gil had been in the wilderness too long. His growing beard was a constant reminder of how long we had been in the wilds.

Winding our way north, we waded the stream about seventeen times. Several times, we didn't even bother to empty our boots, but squished along with water inside. Our feet now were blistered and swollen, with wrinkled water-soaked skin. My shoulders were raw from my packstraps.

AN ARCTIC GROUND SQUIRREL CROUCHED JUST
TWO FEET FROM US

I BEGAN TO WONDER IF GIL HAD BEEN IN THE
WILDERNESS TOO LONG

On about the eleventh crossing, I followed Gil closely. I stretched for a last long step to reach the opposite shore and caught my foot on a submerged willow root.

"Oh, no!" Gil looked around just in time to see me measure my length in the soft deep mud, my heavy pack pinning me down.

My hand had caught in my binocular strap when I instinctively reached out to protect myself in the fall, so I had pitched forward on my face. I wore a muddy mask and was plastered in front from head to toe.

Thoroughly disgusted with my clumsiness, feeling miserable and messy, cold and tired, I just stood there for awhile. Then I straggled over to Gil.

"What a mess. Come on, I'll help you clean up. You can't travel that way." Solicitously, my husband took my pack and led the way to some boulders, where the stream was clear.

"Let's peel off your muddy clothes. While you wash up, I'll rinse them out for you." To save weight on our trip, I had taken no extra jeans.

I stripped. Gil took my clothes to the stream while I started washing up in the cold creek.

"Hurry. That wind is cold!" I shivered, wishing I had brought along a change of clothing.

Gil washed everything and wrung out the water. I put them back on.

"Ugh. This feels awful! They cling."

Hiking on the gravel bars was better walking, an easier grade than the other route, but I was beginning to wonder if it was worth it. I was annoyed to have the clinging wet jeans restrict my leg movements. After a few more stream crossings, I was ready to try the cotton-grass route again.

We made a rest stop and ate supper while four Violet-green Swallows darted back and forth over the stream.

We climbed a low bluff to get the lay of the land. Ahead, the creek made a wide oxbow bend. Across was the pingo where we had gone fishing. We had about six more miles of traveling to get back to our base camp.

Black billowy clouds loomed up over the mountain to the southwest, threatening rain. We decided to take a short-cut to some Feltleaf Willows a mile away by the pingo. By going across the cottongrass, we hoped to reach the willows before the storm struck. Soon—trapped in exasperating tussocks again! Again we tried stepping on tops of the clumps—then between. There was no easy way. We just stumbled through, discouraged, laboring uphill with our wearisome loads. My thin collar bones were bleeding from the constant shifting of the pack-straps. That one mile of tussocks seemed like ten.

We straggled into the willows near the pingo just as large raindrops spattered on the gravel. Then the rain came down in earnest. Hastily, we threw a thin plastic over some horizontal branches, weighted the edges with stones and crept into our improvised haven. Catching our breaths, we ate some candy and nuts—the last food we had with us—and watched the rain.

We now knew we need not wade the stream again, so we put on our last pairs of dry socks. What a comfort, after the abuse our feet had taken. The soles of our shoepacs were getting so thin we could feel the rough stones.

When the shower was over, we again followed the stream. More Spotted Sandpipers bobbed and confronted us with their incessant shrill "Peet-peeeet-peet! Pee-weet, pee-weeeet!" Those noisy little birds were

SPOTTED SANDPIPER
They defended territories along lower Loon Creek

conspicuous at about one-mile intervals along the gravel bars, to about three miles below Loon Lake, where the bars ended. There were no tattlers below the rim, but tattlers replaced the Spotted Sandpipers on the streams above the lake.

Ominous clouds were darkening, so we took little time to rest. We worked our way up steeply, toward the rocky rim of the lake. Ploughing through thick willows and alders, we followed the tracks of a moose that had traveled north toward camp during our absence. The safety of our camp had been at the back of our minds all the time we were gone. We were anxious to learn if it had been ransacked.

Reaching the rim at last, we looked for our camp at the far end. With binoculars, we could just barely see our tent, two miles away. Thankful to find it still standing, we hoped our food and supplies were still intact.

Turbulent black clouds boiled over the valley behind us. Rain-streaks shrouded the flats, motivating our haste as we proceeded along the rocky west shore. The water level of the lake had risen, forcing us onto steeper rocks.

The large loon rode out in the middle of the lake. The gulls and terns came to meet us, and surprisingly, they did not scold. They escorted us the rest of the way. I like to think they missed us.

Wearily, we trudged across the swollen streams and arrived at camp at ten in the evening, immensely relieved to find our camp had not been molested. Ten minutes after our arrival, a cloudburst hit, but we didn't care. Snugly, we sat in the shelter, gobbling up large chunks of Gil's bread with margarine, while a deafening rainstorm beat on the plastic roof of the shelter.

Dashing through the downpour to our Klepper tent, we curled into our sleeping bag and listened to the pounding rain beat a drumroll on the canvas over our heads. But not for long. Sleep deafened us.

Chapter XII

A Week in the Cocoon

> *Here we find nature to be the circum-
> stance to dwarf every other circum-
> stance.*

JULY 18TH, WE WOKE UP IN OUR TENT AT LOON LAKE WITH
the rain still beating a tattoo over our heads. We turned
over and went back to sleep until hunger drove Gil out
to brave the storm in wool underwear, wool pants and
army field pants. He announced it was 36 degrees. I
snuggled deeper into the sleeping bag.

Finally my own hunger drove me out of the warm
cocoon and I joined Gil in the shelter. He had a roaring
fire going, and hot coffee for instant cheer. Heavy low
clouds augured more bad weather and it began to snow
while we took turns frying pancakes for breakfast. We
rigged tarps to close off the front of the plastic shelter,
sealing off the openings to prevent a cold draft on our
feet. We kept the primus burning for added warmth.

After our exertions of the day before, we were content
to remain inactive while waiting out the storm. The clear
plastic let in abundant light. I was writing. Gil was reading Stefansson's *Mysteries of the Arctic*. Aloud, he shared
with me the story of the ill-fated Andree expedition, of
how a primus emitting carbon monoxide in an airtight
tent probably caused the demise of the entire party.

I rushed to let fresh air into our sealed shelter. Subsequently, I made it a point to ventilate at intervals.

At 4:30 P.M., still snowing, the temperature had dropped to 32 degrees. Snow whitened the peaks. Streams were roaring high on both sides of camp. Waves of the lake lapped closer to camp every hour.

Baby birds, out of their nests, crying in the snow all around. Poor baby birds!

"It says here that lupines are poisonous to eat!" Gil exclaimed. He was reading *Alaska Wildflower Trails*, a booklet by Helen White. We gazed at each other incredulously, remembering those we had eaten at Hunt Fork.

Retiring to the Klepper with the primus, we spent a cozy evening taking turns reading aloud to each other. Gil hit the canvas periodically, to make the snow slide down. When we looked out before going to bed, it was still snowing and 32 degrees. The tattler flew up from the snow-covered rocks to look at us just before we zipped close the flap of the tent.

Snowflakes were still drifting down the next morning. There were several inches of snow on the ground. Winter in July. The sheep lay on the snowy ledges, unperturbed. White-crowns and Fox Sparrows were singing from the snow-covered bushes. Then the Tree Sparrow added his merry tune.

"If the birds feel like singing in this weather," Gil remarked, "I don't think we should complain."

Checking our water-level gauge, we found the lake had risen twelve inches since our return from Hunt Fork. Added to the twelve inches it had risen while we were gone, that meant there were only five feet to go before our shelter would be flooded.

KLEPPER TENT—OUR BEDROOM
A July snowstorm. We spent a cozy evening reading aloud to each other

JULY SNOWSTORM
Fluffy snowflakes drifted down the rest of the day to blanket the roof of the shelter.

Birds flitted busily through the snowy bushes as the sun came out to dazzle the snowscape. We wore sunglasses while taking quick baths in 45 degree temperature. With my hands freezing in icy water, I washed some clothes before it clouded up and turned cold again. Then it began to rain, washing the snow away at the lower elevations.

We were now marooned on our triangular island. With streams running so high on both sides of camp, we didn't care to wade the swift icy water to get across. We spent the rest of the day reading, first in the shelter, then in the Klepper.

Next morning, rain was pounding the canvas. Looking out, we saw Upper Loon Creek running wild, flooding its banks. Water was only a foot below our camp level. We talked about moving camp off the island, across the rampaging creek.

"That will be a last resort," Gil decided. "I don't see how I could stand up against the force of the current. Besides, that water is cold!"

The highest ground of our island, two feet higher than camp, was about forty feet west. Moving the Klepper there would give us a reprieve. But the shelter would be too complicated to move.

The rain almost stopped, to give us hope. The streams should go down. We stared with awful fascination as the water came closer and closer to camp and debated whether to move the Klepper before we went to bed. But the rain seemed to be letting up, so we decided to see what the morrow would bring.

The roaring of water jarred me into consciousness. Weird sounds like strong winds tearing through a forest. Rocks tumbling in the stream bed, the sound intensified because our ears were in contact with the ground through our air pillows. We jumped up. It was one A.M.

Looking out, we saw water raging forty feet from our tent. We dressed hurriedly and went outside. The muddy brown torrents were actually *above* the level of our bed. It seemed the water was rushing so fast it didn't have time to turn toward our camp. It was still raining. The unruffled terns flew over, rasping softly in a friendly tiff. The tattlers pa-leeped and flew around over the maelstrom. Where were their gray chicks? Were they bobbing in the water? Since they can swim like ducklings, they would be at home in the turbulent waters.

From my diary:

Water all around, getting higher and higher. It seems inevitable. Sooner or later, we will have to move camp. But if it would stop raining altogether, and the sun came out, maybe we would be all right.

The poor robin by camp. Her island is smaller still. The raging streams have engulfed the area, only a foot of ground at the base of her nesting tree. There she sits, huddling, brooding her

TATTLER CHICK
They swim like ducklings and are right at home in turbulent floodwaters

young, which are ready to leave the nest. If, in their first flight, they do not fly over the flood, they won't have a chance.

The water is inching up as we watch.

Noon. It's starting to rain hard again. We sit in the shelter and try to forget (for the moment) about the rain. We read to each other. It continues raining.

✿   ✿   ✿

Gil began building dikes to hold back the rushing torrent. Some water trickled through, so he dug ditches to divert it. The water was now lapping over the last few inches—seeping through by the tent.

Deciding it was time to move the Klepper, I started to pack up. I deflated the air mattress, packed the sleeping bag and our clothes. We had specimens hanging and two plant presses full of plants to be dried. Plants which had been dried and packaged were gathering dampness again. Everything went into large plastic bags, protection against soaking.

The rain poured until four o'clock, then eased off and practically stopped. Gil figured that since we were near the head of the valley, the runoff would occur quickly. The flood should crest at six o'clock, and stay high for hours. We had hopes of saving the shelter.

Gil kept diking, desperately trying to hold back the water, but it began running toward the shelter and tent. We moved everything from the Klepper into the shelter, struck the tent and moved it to the two-foot-higher ground. After re-establishing our sleeping quarters, we placed flat stones over the mud at our doorstep. It began to rain again. Gil built another dike.

From my diary:

6 P.M.   Gil's dikes are holding back the flood or the water would be pouring into the shelter by now. This is the crest, we

hope. If the water rises another four inches, we could not hold it.
Most of our food is in cans on the ground. If the dikes break, the
willows would slow down the current enough so the cans would
not be swept away.

8 P.M. We had supper. The water level is holding. We see
some blue sky overhead as we look through the plastic roof.

9 P.M. The storm is abating. The streams seem to be holding
their own—or even lowering by an inch. To the south, weather
looks better. We now have hopes the crisis will soon pass. If it
rains again, it will be worse than ever. The lake rose 18 inches
today.

Lake has about four feet to go to be full. Then the overflow
at other end should be effective to maintain a constant level.
(But that would be too late.)

11 P.M The crest has passed. The creek is down two inches—
still being held by the dikes. We long for sunny weather, so we
can wash up and dry out.

Robin is still brooding her young amidst the rampaging flood.

⚹　⚹　⚹

We went to bed and lay listening to the roaring flood
waters, nearer now. Strange wild cacophony of gur-
glings, swishings, moanings, groanings. Rocks tumbling,
bumping, grinding in the stream bed just outside our
tent.

Woke to rain. Just what we didn't need! We put our
heads deep into the sleeping bag and went back to sleep,
hoping it would go away. Two more hours. Still raining. Can't hear the birds over the roaring water sounds
—a weird wild sort of music, like Stravinsky's.

Gil looked out to the main channel and saw the stream
had actually lowered about six inches from the crest.
Rain seemed to be easing off. Things looked better—until
we looked the other way and noticed the lake level was
still rising, inexorably rising. What a dismal scene.
Heavy black clouds shrouded the peaks. Water streamed
in torrents down the mountain slopes. The lichens, act-

ing like sponges, were saturated and could hold no more. Everything was soaked down to the barrier of permafrost, the water *had* to run off. Water cascaded down the ravines. Waterfalls roared down every gully. Water drenched the valley. It all discharged into the lake.

The shelter looked uninviting and forlorn—utterly bedraggled. Dripping olive-drab tarps drearily hung over the front. Inside, soggy socks and jackets hung limply next to us. Rain pattered steadily on the plastic roof.

The wood fire flared up brightly, to give us warmth, cheer and hot food. Gil cooked extra goodies, like ham omelet and cheesecake pie (no-bake), to boost our morale. I entertained by reading aloud. Then I played "our" song on the harmonica—"The Bear Went Over the Mountain."

For two more days, we were shelter-bound, waiting out the rain. The stream continued to drop, the lake

FLOOD!

Plastic shelter on the right. High water forced us to move the Klepper to the highest point on our island (only two feet higher) to the right and out of the picture.

level to rise. We looked up to the sheep. They had moved down to lie under shelves in shallow caves. They too, seemed to be waiting for the rains to cease.

We saw the loon out on the lake. The tattler adults were there, but we didn't see the chicks, who were somewhere down on the bleak shore. The gulls flew over and were promptly chased away. The terns calmly hunted for their young, safely hidden somewhere near their peninsula. The robin scrunched down tightly over her restless young.

One morning, we woke to dazzling light. Glorious, unbelievable sunshine! Another springtime after a siege of winter. The tent glowed with warmth as we dressed, but we hurried to go out and bask in the blessed brilliance, under peaks glistening with snow.

"No wonder primitives worshipped the sun," Gil said reverently. "It was their only source of heat and light."

Joyously we bathed, shampooed and washed clothes.

ROBIN ADULT, WITH A NEST NEAR OUR CAMP
She scrunched down to keep her young safe in the nest until the flood was over.

Plant presses and specimens were brought out into the sun. Then jackets and boots. Then sleeping bag and blankets.

Two of the baby robins tried their wobbly wings on their first precarious flights. The stubby-tailed fledglings landed, shakily, but safely, at the edge of their small island. One remained in the nest, timidly peering over the edge. It took him two more days to muster up enough gumption to enter the brave new world. Then he landed on a branch just below the nest. We dubbed him "Retardo."

ROBIN YOUNG, FIFTEEN DAYS OLD
He stayed in the nest two days after his nest mates had fledged. We called him "Retardo."

Chapter XIII

Halcyon Days

> *Therefore is nature glorious with form, color and motion.*

WHEN THE HAWK CHICKS WERE TWELVE DAYS OLD, WE PAID them another visit. With a climbing rope, we angled up the slopes to get above the nest. One of the parent hawks saw us coming and went to warn the other. They both hovered over us, crying. I felt terrible for disturbing them.

The three still-downy young lay sprawled flat in the nest apparently sound asleep. They had grown at an

ROUGH-LEGGED HAWK CHICKS TWELVE DAYS OLD
These had the highest pesticide content of all the birds tested

astonishing rate, were nearly half grown and covered with a thick coat of light gray fuzz, like sheep wool. From the top of the cliff, I belayed Gil while he climbed down to the aerie to get pictures. The hawklets lay still as death until Gil touched one gently with a short stick. With startling suddenness, it sat back on its haunches and opened its fierce-looking little hooked beak threateningly. His nestmates didn't move. Gil touched another chick and got the same sudden reaction. It popped up like a jack-in-the-box.

The chicks had unusually large dark eyes, with black smudges in front, like eyeshadow. The sides of their beaks still retained the yellow edging typical of all baby birds. They were remarkably paunchy, reminding us of small children with rickets.

Two freshly killed Tundra Voles, like overgrown field mice, lay on the sticks. Another interesting feature of the aerie was a fresh green willow branch recently placed there. Hawks and eagles have the puzzling habit of decorating their nests with fresh green branches throughout the nesting season. We believe it adds to the camouflage. Certainly, because of the greenery, this large stick nest was harder to spot from across the canyon.

After taking pictures of the young hawks, Gil added another insult by stealing the two rodents for pesticide samples. The frantic parent Rough-legs, expecting their children to be murdered, cried and flew from one side of the ravine to the other. To relieve their anxieties, we wasted no time in leaving the vicinity and returning to the valley.

The tattlers moved in close to camp with their three active "teenagers." The parents, getting tamer every day, discovered that our cloths-drying pole made an ex-

ROUGH-LEGGED HAWK CHICK TWELVE DAYS OLD
His tummy bulged like that of a baby with rickets, and he wore black
smudges in front of his eyes—like eyeshadow.

TUNDRA VOLES
While visiting the hawk nest, adding insult to injury, Gil stole the two rodents for pesticide samples.

cellent perch. We had to shoo them away in order to hang up our clothes.

A tern hovered briefly, dipped into the water and came up with a wiggly three-inch fish. While circling overhead, the tern adeptly tossed the fingerling into the air a few times, like a juggler, to get a proper hold on it before settling on the shore to gulp it down.

We found the terns' downy young—only one—sitting like a pink-footed plump gray gosling on the rocks at the water's edge. The doting parents spelled each other in baby-sitting the ten-day-old, one keeping watch while the other fished. Never was the tern-child alone. He was their pride and joy.

"That chick gets more attention than any other youngster in the neighborhood," I commented as I watched

THE TERNS' PRIDE AND JOY
Since they think he's so great, I'm going to call him "Precious." Gil gave
a snort of disgust.

the close-knit tern family on the shore. "Since they think he's so great, I'm going to name him 'Precious.'"

Gil gave a snort of disgust. "It's not scientific to give your study subject a sentimental name."

That did it. More to tease Gil than for any other reason, I called the tern chick "Precious" from then on. Actually Precious had a rather stupid appearance as he sat dully on the gray rocks, attended by his beautiful solicitous parents.

As I watched, one of the terns cocked its head to look up, then started rasping an alarm. With amazing single-mindedness, the gulls teamed up with the tern in wild protestations. They flew skyward, climbing an invisible spiral staircase to the top of the mountain, in pusuit of two Golden Eagles soaring over the valley.

To make the day perfect, there was not a breath of wind. For the first time, there were no waves on the lake.

From my diary:

We crossed over Tern Peninsula and looked at the lake—smooth as glass—gorgeous and nearly full to the brim, like we had never seen. A lovely mountain jewel. We were spellbound by the splendid reflections of Loon Peak . . . the soft shadings of greens, browns and grays reversed on the mirrored surface. This day has been such a perfect one, and now this gift. We were grateful. The flowers—saxifrages, *Epilobium,* Jacob's Ladder—and the three dimensional lacey lichens refreshed by the rain. We kept remarking, "How beautiful!" and "How lovely!"

❀   ❀   ❀

Five black Surf Scoters with bright yellow noses flew swift as arrows past us in single file formation. Time and again they circled low over the glassy surface, keeping in formation like dark chorus girls in the Ice Follies, in a remarkable exhibition just for us. Then they settled down on the lake. The show was over.

WE CROSSED OVER AND LOOKED AT LOON LAKE
It was as smooth as glass—like we had never seen, a lovely mountain jewel

Moments later, a north wind sprang up to erase all the reflections from the lake. For many days, all during the rainy period, the wind had been from the south. Now our hopes were high for the good weather to continue.

Midnight found us at the south end of the lake to investigate the overflow situation. Although water was not pouring over the rim, raging torrents surged through the rocks. The lake level was holding, even going down slightly. We were relieved, for unless it rained again, our camp would not be flooded.

Sitting on rocks at the shore, we gazed toward camp two miles away. The ever-present loon looked lonely out on the lake. The tiny island was in the foreground.

"I just saw a duck sneak onto the island," Gil announced. "She probably has a nest there. I wish we had a boat."

"Why not build a raft?" As soon as I said it, I realized there was no wood available and a raft could not be built out of willows. "How about the air mattress? If the wind dies down, one of us could ride out on it. I'm smaller, so I should go."

"*If* the wind died down. But it could come up again fast and blow you around like a leaf. This is a big lake, it's deep. And the water is cold."

"We could make some little paddles."

"You wouldn't be able to control it against a wind. But I have an idea. If we tied a light line on it, I could always pull you back if you were blown the wrong way. It wouldn't work at all, of course, unless you had a favorable wind."

The next day, we lucked out. Another dazzling day, with a slight south breeze that would blow me right to the island. We tramped to the south end with the air mattress, two little paddles whittled out of a small board, and a couple hundred yards of strong very lightweight nylon line. I also had a plastic cup with an airtight lid, some large strong plastic bags, and rubber bands.

The double air mattress was blown up as tightly as possible. If part of the raft was punctured, I could hang onto the two attached air pillows.

"You'll probably get wet. Just be sure to hang on if you get dunked." Gil rigged a harness around the raft and tied the line to it.

In warm sunshine, I changed into my climbing shorts, put my heavy pants and jacket in plastic bags and sealed them up along with the plastic cup, and I tied all to the harness of the raft.

"Hey, the breeze has changed. Now its from the north. But if you stay in the lee of the island, you can paddle over." Gil carried the air mattress to the water's edge.

Standing beside it, careful not to tip it, I sat down in the middle with my back against the air pillows.

"How about that? I hardly got wet."

Gil handed me the paddles and I floated away, feeling like Cleopatra on her barge. Gil paid out the line while I bobbed out onto the big lake. After traveling on foot all summer, this smooth ride in the warm sun was sheer luxury.

Five Oldsquaw females flying in formation approached low and fast over the water. They nearly collided with me.

"Ow," they said, then veered away.

I soon reached the island, grabbed a small willow and pulled myself ashore. The rocky island, a thirty- by seventy-foot oval, was partly covered with shin-high wil-

VIVIAN RIDING THE AIR MATTRESS TO THE ISLAND
After searching a second time around, she flushed an incubating harlequin under a low bush.

lows and birch. Making a systematic search around the shore, under the bushes and around the rocks, I could find no nest. I started around the second time and leaned over a prostrate willow about three feet from the shore. Gray feathers shot out from under the bush. A female Harlequin slid into the water. Again I saw six creamy eggs cozily cradled in dark gray down. A lovely picture, but I was immediately sorry I had found it. The little duck had concealed it so perfectly she deserved to keep her secret.

Reluctantly, I stole one of her eggs and sealed it in the plastic cup, cushioning it with moss. This I resealed in a large plastic bag, blowing in some extra air before tying it to the raft. If it went overboard, it would still be safe.

The wind died down completely before Gil started

pulling me back to shore. The Harlequin had been wait-ing. She swam over near me, then went through a splashing broken-wing ruse, and I let her lead me away from *her* island. The raft ride again was pure delight, and I gloried in the rare balmy Arctic day.

The fine weather sent us exploring and photographing the plants on the rocky peninsula. Climbing over large black-lichen-covered blocks in sheer exuberance, we scrambled across the top.

"Notice those rocks over there. They look different. Not so much lichen on them. Maybe a grizzly turned them over."

I went to investigate.

"This is a den or something. Come take a look." I climbed down inside and found a square pit, deep enough for a man, with huge flat slabs for a roof.

Gil looked in. "That's no den. This was man-made a

HARLEQUIN DUCK NEST

One egg removed for a sample. Again I saw creamy eggs cozily cradled in dark gray down.

I HANDED GIL MY TROPHY—THE HARLEQUIN EGG

long time ago. See how the lichen stops where the rocks overlap. Some Eskimo made this."

What was it for? A cache? We thought not. It would be so easy for a grizzly to raid it.

"I think some primitive had his home here." I pictured a stone-age North American living in this exact spot.

"It probably was a hunting blind," my prosaic husband thought. "Pretty small for a house."

"Why did he go to all this heavy work just for a blind when there are so many rocks to hide behind? Their dwellings *were* small, so they could heat them with a lamp."

Whether the pit was a cache, a blind or a dwelling, we could not decide. The lichens told us it was made long, long ago.

VIVIAN IN AN ANCIENT ESKIMO CACHE
South end of Loon Lake

THE LICHENS TOLD US IT WAS MADE A LONG TIME AGO
Whether the pit was a cache, a hunting blind, or a dwelling, we could not decide.

Chapter XIV

"Never Run from a Grizzly"

The solitary places do not seem quite lonely.

WE HAD SEEN NO GRIZZLIES FOR A WEEK. WE KNEW THEY were around though, from the signs of them on all sides of camp. But we were gaining more confidence every day. We didn't spend so much time glassing the slopes or looking over our shoulders.

One day, Gil and I sat eating lunch in the shelter, waiting out another sudden summer storm. Lightning played zig-zaggedly across the peaks, thunder reverberated through the valley, rain and wind slammed us from the north. Then the storm ended as abruptly as it had started. The sun came out and we emerged from our crude plastic palace, put on tennis shoes, and went down to the beach.

The rocks steamed in the sun. The tattler family foraged busily, parents pa-leeping, constantly riding herd on their wandering offspring. One tern hovered over our heads, the other was baby-sitting Precious near the water.

We made a game of hopping over various sections of the stream flowing into the lake, trying to keep our tennis shoes from getting wet. Rocks started sliding and rolling noisily down the slopes of Loon Peak. Looking up, we could not see the sheep that had dislodged them. Probably hidden from view.

Much of the time, we were gung-ho to go exploring, but today we planned no hike. We sauntered west along the rocky shore—just dawdling, enjoying the sun, the fresh air, the scenery, the birds. The whole world was our oyster. Wilderness living was giving us a whole new sense of values. Materialism was in the distant past. It no longer mattered that we owned a comfortable middle-class home in Lake Oswego, Oregon. *This* was really living!

"Look at that big pile of nice clean driftwood. It's time to bake bread again." Gil started gathering up an armload of the polished white sticks to take back to camp.

The wood was wet, and I wasn't inspired to help. It was fun just to loaf along, taking it easy. I would help him later.

"Aren't you coming?" Gil started toward camp.

TERN PARENT BABY-SITTING "PRECIOUS"
One parent was constantly by his side. Together they stuffed him with fish

WILDERNESS LIVING WAS GIVING US A WHOLE
NEW SENSE OF VALUES
Materialism was in the distant past

"Naw. That robin up ahead is carrying food for its young. The nest must be close. I'll just mosey along, pretending I'm not following it. I'd like to find one more nest."

Moving slowly, not looking directly at it, I followed the robin, climbing up the gentle slope about seventy-five feet. The robin gave me the slip and disappeared. Clever. I really didn't care—my tennis shoes were not adequate for the terrain anyway. I sat down and basked in the warm sun.

Casually, I glanced up and for a wild moment I couldn't believe what I saw. From habit, I grabbed the binoculars hanging round my neck. Yegods! A bear! A grizzly down at the shore. And coming right at me! Through the glasses, a monstrous shaggy head with little gleaming eyes practically filled the field of vision.

I don't remember starting, but I suddenly realized I was running, panic-stricken away from the bear who was chasing me.

Three hundreds yards ahead, on the other side of the willows, was camp—and Gil. Enveloped in terror, I plunged madly through the cottongrass, paralleling the shore. Like a caribou, I bounded over the tussocks. The bear was not far behind. Then, sickeningly, I remembered. I should not be running.

"Never run from a grizzly," a ranger once told us. "Face him and scream—loud as you can!"

"Help! Bear! Bear! Bear!" Wild shrieks rent the air, but I could not stop running. I ran like the wind, threading between tussocks, jumping through bushes, spurred by sheer terror.

"Help! Bear!" I screeched at the top of my lungs.

I stumbled, regained my balance, and reached the willows sobbing.

Everything blurred. I rounded the willows, stumbling, splashing into the creek. I think I fell down. Then I saw Gil—calmly setting up the camera on the tripod. I collapsed in his arms.

"My gosh!" Gil exclaimed. "I didn't know you were in trouble. Just now, I heard you scream 'bear,' and I thought you wanted me to take his picture."

Limp as a rag, I sank down with a moan, too weak to be mad at him.

"There it goes, around the shore." Gil pointed. The bear had come to the willows and now was running the other way. It followed the shore the way it had appeared, traversed the slope and disappeared over the ridge.

"Here, have some coffee. Tell me what happened."

The coffee scalded my throat, which was raw from screaming, and I noticed that my clothes were soaking wet.

"Just let me lie down and rest forever."

"How did that grizzly get so close to camp without our seeing it?" Gil scratched his head. "They come from all directions."

Then we remembered thinking that the rolling rocks we had heard earlier had been dislodged by sheep. When we looked up, we had been looking for white mountain sheep, not a grizzly, whose color would blend in with the slope. We started glassing again—in every direction.

Chapter XV

Lupus and the Dall King

*Every hour and season yields its trib-
ute of delight.*

ONE SPARKLING JULY MORNING GIL WAS FRYING FISH FOR
breakfast on an outdoor rock "stove" while I stayed in
the open tent to write. With background music provided
by Fox and Tree Sparrows, I worked on nest records.
The terns were conversing softly overhead in raspy whis-
pers.

"Time to get up," my chef called. "Breakfast will soon
be ready."

I took a pan of water outside and, leaning over, I
splashed cold water on my face. Gil was dishing up the
food. As I reached for a towel, my eyes strayed over Gil's
shoulder. A pair of yellowish-brown eyes were gazing
intently at us over some low bushes near the stream.
The almond-shaped eyes were set in a broad, gray canine
face.

"Sled dog!" I thought. Company coming—Eskimos!

Then it came to me. I breathed to Gil in an awed
whisper, "Don't move. There's a wolf!"

"Where?" Gil looked up, wide-eyed.

"Right behind you—in camp—there!"

Gil spun around.

Like an apparition, the wolf vanished. A moment

later, it was staring at us again from fifteen feet farther away. It had crossed a section of the stream.

Gil stooped and ran for his camera. The movement made the animal uneasy. He dropped into the creek bed north of camp and reappeared a couple hundred yards to the east. On a slight rise, *Canis lupus* turned and stood watching us as we returned his stares with equal fascination.

This Arctic wolf looked very much like a large German Shepherd dog, only with shorter rounded ears and longer legs. Rear legs held in a slight crouch, he looked powerful but rangy and very thin, as though he had traveled many miles without food. Lupus was hungry.

The wolf glanced north up the valley several times, as if expecting a companion. But we were the object of his consuming curiosity as he was ours.

"Few people are privileged to see a real wolf in the wild." Gil's voice revealed his excitement. "I don't think

THIS ARCTIC WOLF LOOKED VERY MUCH LIKE A
GERMAN SHEPHERD DOG
He turned and stood watching us

this one has experienced man before, otherwise he would high-tail it out of here. In these parts, wolves are hunted for their hides—and a $50 bounty."

"It doesn't seem right."

"No, it doesn't. Biologists believe the wolf is important to the survival of a healthy caribou herd, but the bounty hunters—and domestic farmers—have managed to convince the politicians that wolves should be exterminated."

Lupus seemed undecided which way to go. After observing us at some length, and with more glances to the north, he started trotting in that direction, changed his mind and headed east again, up the lower slope of Ursus. From a vantage point a quarter mile away, he sat down on his haunches and gave us his undivided attention. We were captivated. These meaningful, magical moments, when we were being regarded by a living, breathing Arctic wolf, were one of the highlights of the summer.

Lupus captured our imagination. What did this wild one think of us? Did he have hunting companions? A family? Was he a lone wolf?

These intelligent animals have developed an interesting social life. They live and hunt in groups, called packs. Their lives revolve around the family. Parent wolves are devoted to each other and to their pups. The mother usually stays with the "kids," while the father works with "uncles" and other members of the pack in organized hunts. Food is brought home to the den by all members of the pack and regurgitated to feed the youngsters.

Food is whatever is available—in this region, usually caribou. Since the weak—the old, extremely young, or the sick—are most easily taken, the strong caribou are left to reproduce. If there are not enough wolves, the caribou population becomes too large, overgrazes, and deteriorates in health. Many starve, for the lichens they graze on are extremely slow growing, sometimes requiring thirty or forty years before they can support caribou again.

All the time Lupus sat looking at us, we stood in rapt attention, as if he had cast a spell over us. Finally he got up and trotted into a gully, his gray color harmonizing with the muted grays and browns of the slope. Like a phantom, he materialized, then disappeared. We saw him. Then we didn't.

"How about breakfast?" Gil said, still awestruck. We had forgotten to eat.

We ate our morning meal, feeling that the wolf's amber eyes were still on us. Because of him, the whole morning seemed brighter. An air of mysticism pervaded the valley.

And we wished him well. If this was his first encounter with man, Lupus had not yet learned the important lesson that man is his enemy. We hoped that next winter, with his associates, he would still be roaming like a gray spectre over the snowy hills and mountains in the long, bitter Arctic night. While northern lights dance overhead, may he always lend enchantment to the land while performing his role in the balance of nature.

*   *   *

Gil and I lived in an interesting community. The tattlers seemed to have accepted us as friends. The clothes-drying pole was still a favorite perch for watching over their young. We had an amicable arrangement. They let us use it occasionally.

The robin-sized tattlers lorded it over the other bird species. It was amusing to watch the cry-baby gulls being evicted by the much smaller tattlers. The gulls always complained as though they were mistreated.

Later in the season, the Baird's Sandpipers came down from the mountains and began feeding in the territory. The tattlers chased them away too, but the tiny Bairds seemed to think it was all fun and games. They just followed the tattlers back to camp and began feeding beside them again.

Once after we had gone to bed, we heard creatures rustling outside the tent. We peeked out to see a pair of Rock Ptarmigan. The male croaked like a frog, much to our amusement. They came regularly after that when we were in the tent and eventually let us approach quite close, if we moved slowly.

The white sheep were nearly always visible on the ledges. Ewes and lambs, in small groups, wandered over

MEW GULL
The crybaby gulls always complained as though they were mistreated

the slopes, but the regal rams favored the sheer west cliffs. There, aloof and safe from predators, they gazed over the valley, like barons surveying their domain. Usually a dozen or more rams rested peacefully when they were not feeding or butting heads. The young rams were constantly having pushing contests, which seemed all in fun. The older rams jousted too, but their games were rougher. Sometimes they back up and, with heads down, rush toward each other with tremendous speed, until their massive horns smash together with a jarring "clack." We could hear them at camp. Once we found evidence that at least one duel had a tragic ending. Skulls with the horns of two old rams were lying side by side at the base of a high, sheer wall.

To the north of Ursus was a peak we dubbed "Aquila," for the Golden Eagles often sported around its summit. It was a U-shaped mountain, facing the afternoon sun, with its arms around a valley. One evening we were

DALL RAMS
Sometimes they jousted, running and smashing their horns together with a loud "clack" we could hear at camp.

DALL RAM HORNS
Evidence that this duel had a tragic ending

LOON LAKE FROM AQUILA PEAK
Loon Peak on right

climbing Aquila Peak, beginning at the lower south ridge. A magnificent ram watched our approach like the king of the mountain he was. The ram climbed ahead of us, and when we stopped to look around and rest, the ram did also. He climbed no faster than we, he stayed just a few hundred yards ahead. Each time we stopped, we saw him lying at ease on the ramparts above, his splendid horns in regal silhouette against the azure sky.

All the way to the summit, his Majesty ascended, unhurriedy, with royal equanimity and grace, as we moved up behind him. Then we saw him resting on his throne— the top of his mountain.

When we finally reached the summit, he was lying quietly on a connecting peak, waiting for us to go by. We continued our traverse of the long U ridge, descending the other arm. Clouds swirled around the peaks as Gil and I looked back to see his Majesty, the King of the

ROCK PTARMIGAN—MALE
After we went to bed, he came around our tent and croaked like a frog

Dalls, in his immaculate white robe, lying serenely on his craggy throne in the sky.

✿   ✿   ✿

Many times we became so engrossed with observing and photographing that we forgot to grizzly-watch. One such time we were prowling through the valley a half-mile north of camp when we came upon a family of Rock Ptarmigan. The hen, in mottled camouflage, stood still and stretched her neck up tall to look at us, while the two-week-old chicks took the cue from her. They made good photographic subjects, because ptarmigan depend on their coloration for concealment and to remain unseen they hold perfectly still. While Gil was taking ptarmigan pictures, I sat on the ground in the warm sun, with my back to the willow brush. Lazily I watched the birds standing like statues in the colorful River Beauty, posing prettily for their portraits.

ROCK PTARMIGAN

The hen, in mottled camouflage, stretched her neck up tall to look at us. The chick took his cue from her.

ROCK PTARMIGAN CHICK
They can fly when a week old, but they usually hold still, depending on concealing coloration.

The following day, we were shocked to find a fresh bear scat where we had lethargically photographed the ptarmigan. If the bear had appeared while we were there, I don't know who would have been more startled, Gil and I or the grizzly.

Another day, we were farther north in a Feltleaf thicket, looking for nests. There we found a few small Downy-sized Woodpecker nest holes about a foot from the ground, the only place the willow trunks were thick enough. One woodpecker had made the mistake of working on too small a willow and had bored through to the opposite side before realizing there was no space for a nest.

A Willow Warbler sang his dry monotonous trill from a willow tip. It was carrying food for young. This elusive warbler from Asia was another challenge for Gil. A

VIVIAN NOTING WOODPECKER SIGN IN A WILLOW
This was north of Loon Lake, far north of tree line. The nest holes were one foot from the ground.

couple of weeks earlier, he had found a Willow Warbler nest by lying for two hours under a tarp watching them. At last one of the diminutive gray birds flew down to a clump of grass. Gil had found a rare nest.

"You stay where you are. Just sit perfectly quiet, and I think I can find the nest. Don't come or call to me." Gil disappeared in the thicket.

I sat down on a mossy hummock under the willows, resigned to a long wait. The warbler trilled in the cool, refreshing air. Delicate Pink Pyrola (*P. grandiflora*) and Monk's Hood bloomed in the yellow moss. A juvenal Northern Shrike, with dark bandit mask, flew up and looked me over, then went on his way clumsily chasing a robin. I heard a family of Gray Jays. We had seen them earlier.

Then I had a premonition. It occurred to me that a

grizzly might come meandering through while I sat there so quietly. Nervously, I wished Gil would hurry. I peered into the brush all around. I listened.

I grew very uneasy. After another half hour, I called to Gil. No answer. I waited. I called again. Still no answer. I listened and kept watching all around. I hated to spoil Gil's chance of finding another rare nest.

At last, I could contain myself no longer. I yelled. Still no answer from Gil. I got up and went through the willows in the direction he had disappeared. I found him just giving up watching the warblers. He had discovered they were feeding young out of the nest. He had not heard me call.

We wandered up the valley a quarter mile farther, out of the willows, and sat on a knoll enjoying the scenery for awhile. When we hiked back through the willows where the warblers were feeding young, we found fresh signs that a grizzly had passed close to where we had

GIL WITH CARIBOU ANTLER
We found it on the tundra in the upper valley

been sitting a short time before. The green plants were just straightening up where the bear's big footpads had pressed them down. He had been in the thicket all the time we were there!

The beast was traveling toward camp. By traversing up the slope to the east, we hoped to bypass him. Then we saw him below, big and blond, busily munching on green peavines *(Astragalus umbellatus)*. We made a wide detour around him and went "home" to camp.

The bear stayed there for three days, gorging in the same locality. We avoided the upper valley, kept alert, and watched to the north. When in the shelter, we were grateful for the transparent plastic, but at bedtime we became philosophical. So far, we had always lucked out.

                              ✿   ✿   ✿

The last of July, Gil was trying some abstract photography by one of the streams while I was preoccupied with camp chores. Suddenly, he gave a loud whoop.

"Yea! Victory at last! Come over here. I have a surprise!"

I ran to join him and saw him slam a headnet down over some riffles in the stream. He caught a little fish less than three inches long.

"What kind is it?"

"I don't know. It looks like a cross between a bullhead and a miniature rock cod. Ugly little critters. I just happened to catch a glimpse of one darting like lightning from under one rock to another."

Gil caught two more of the odd little fish, all about the same size. We took them to camp to weigh and measure. The largest was three and a quarter inches (80mm) long. We would use them for pesticide specimens.

It was my duty to prepare them for drying. I cut into the abdomen of the largest one, and was shocked to see a flat, wide white tapeworm wiggle and unfold itself out of the fish's abdominal cavity. The parasite was 150mm long—nearly twice as long as its host. In the other two fish I found tapeworms also. The thought of the terns, gulls and tattlers feeding on these parasite-ridden fish disturbed us. We wondered if they digested the worms, or if they, too, became unwitting hosts for the parasites.

Later, with his bare hands Gil caught some more of the miniature fish. The largest was 85mm long and contained an unusually large tapeworm. Gil placed the fish, with its parasite, in a small bottle of alcohol to take back for identification.*

One of the most abundant ducks of the region is the little Harlequin. After the eggs are laid, the females rebuff the gaudy males and get along without them. The rejected males then seek solace by assembling in little groups to while away the rest of the summer in bachelorhood. Free as the breeze, flotillas of divorced males ride on the lake during moult.

Domestic duties are left to the females. The last part of July, the hens appear on the lakes with from three to six gray ducklings each. These downy young are true water-babies.

---

*We gave the bottled small fish, with parasite, to Dr. L. G. Swartz, Department of Biological Sciences, University of Alaska. Dr. Swartz informed us that the specimen was a Sculpin, which creeps upstream from under one rock to another. They can be found in the smallest mountain streams. Undoubtedly the fish had worked their way through the rocks where water flowed from Loon Lake to the lower creek.

The tapeworms *(Ligula intestinalis)* are parasites of Cormorants and Red-breasted Mergansers. Sculpins are intermediate hosts, carrying them in their abdominal cavities, not in their intestinal tracts. Terns and gulls digest the worms, but Cormorants or Red-breasted Mergansers carry them, if ingested, in their intestinal tracts, where they continue developing.

SCULPINS
The largest fish in Loon Lake and the objects of Gil's frustrations

With amazement, we watched the female Harlequin and her young progress up the swift and turbulent mountain streams. In single file, mother leading, they clung to the rocks in the bottom of the stream beds and *walked upstream,* sometimes with heads under water, sometimes above. How they could travel against the force of the swirling currents was beyond our understanding. When going downstream, like so many bobbing gray corks they gaily rode the cascades in a wild, swirling roller-coaster trip.

We did not often see caribou, but their fresh tracks on the trails showed up all through the summer. Occasionally one would wander through the valley, and in August we observed with great pleasure the magnificent bucks in their new fall capes.

Once on an all-day hiking trip to the northwest, we rambled along a delightful alpine brook until we reached a deep cirque gouged out of the north side of Loon Peak.

OCCASIONALLY, A CARIBOU WOULD WANDER
THROUGH THE VALLEY
A caribou doe in August

We found three entrancing little lakes nestled at the base of steep cliffs, with white sheep lying on the ledges. They looked so peaceful there, we didn't disturb them. We call those the "Dall Lakes."

We looked for Hoary Marmots, which live in colonies under large rocks in the mountains. These shy rodents would not let us get close to them. They always have a sentinel who whistles a shrill alarm if danger threatens. Eskimos like to use their fur for parkas.

IN AUGUST, THE MALES HAD THEIR NEW FALL CAPES

HOARY MARMOT
They live in colonies under large rocks in the mountains. There is always a
sentinel, who gives a shrill whistle if alarmed.

Chapter XVI

The Calendar Flips Forward — and, Luckily, Back

> In the wilderness, (we) find something more dear and connate.

IN EARLY AUGUST, BERRIES BEGAN RIPENING ON THE KNOLLS. The rather insipid black Crowberries and Bearberries provided a feast for the birds and small mammals, but the luscious Blueberries and Ground Cranberries were relished by all of us. Gil picked the Blueberries, which are like Oregon Huckleberries, and served them fresh with Dream Whip. The brilliant red Cranberries were cooked and served with meat. Cloudberries were not abundant—these pale juicy morsels ripened later. All these berries were on ground-hugging plants which matted parts of the tundra. Red Currants, on the other hand, hung like translucent drops of blood on taller bushes below the rim of the lake, in a spot protected from the north winds.

Along with the birds large and small enjoying the banquet of berries on the knolls came the family of ravens to partake of the heady fruit. These rascals were the comedians of the community, and as they pranced clownishly on Tern Peninsula, acting tipsy, we wondered if some of the fruit was fermented. Amused by their antics and droll "talk," we stood by, imitating their articulations.

They got the message that we wanted to be friends and became quite tame. The friendliest one we dubbed "Nevermore." He looked comical with his huge, ebony Roman nose and the glint in his eye seemed to reveal that he thought we looked ridiculous too.

Ravens, like crows, can live to be sixty or seventy years old. They are among the most intelligent of birds, ranking close to domestic dogs in problem-solving tests. They make interesting and affectionate pets and will attach themselves not only to members of the human family, but to other pets of the family as well. We have seen a raven strolling along the tundra in company with a grizzly, the strange duo traveling side by side over the dry knolls. The raven walked most of the time and only hopped short distances when necessary to keep up with his companion. Another time, a raven traveled in company with a wolf. No doubt both species benefit from this relationship, but if tamed ravens form attachments with

THE RAVEN, "NEVERMORE"
He came to eat the ripened berries on the dry knolls. This wise old bird could be sixty or even seventy years old.

other species, *it is possible* that wild ones develop an affection of sorts for other wild species.

We have observed ravens play more than any other bird species. In the updrafts off the tops of the peaks, they have the most fun performing barrel-rolls and loop-the-loops and playing roller-coaster games.

On our last visit to the hawk chicks, Gil went down the rope to photograph them again. They were twenty-one days old.

"Since this is the last time we'll see these chicks, you should go down to have a good look at them too. They're pretty cute." Gil sat down and prepared to belay me while I climbed down to the aerie.

The roly-poly young were big fuzzy blobs nearly full-grown, with their primary feathers just emerging from their sheaths. The hawklets looked menacing when I crouched on the stick nest beside them. Open fierce-

A ROLY-POLY ROUGH-LEGGED HAWK CHICK
TWENTY-ONE DAYS OLD
A fresh, green birch branch to the right of the chick

looking hooked beaks threatened me. Their talons gripped the sticks of the aerie.

I began to talk softly to them in a cooing voice. The chicks closed their beaks and tipped their heads to look at me inquisitively. Their unfriendly attitude changed to one of appealing juvenile curiosity.

I climbed up to Gil and we left the Rough-legged Hawks in their mountain hideaway. We talked about all the hazards these young birds would face as soon as they began their migration south.* Many people are ignorant of the laws which protect these beneficial Raptores which feed mostly on rodents.

Among the rodents we collected for specimens was the interesting Singing Vole—the Hay Mouse. Our attention had been attracted to a tiny rodent squeaking repeatedly in the cottongrass. It proved to be a Singing Vole (*Microtus miurus*), discovered by Dr. Adolph Murie in Mt. Mckinley Park. We had seen their piles of "hay" (mostly willow and fireweed leaves) which were stacked neatly under willows or next to rocks for drying and then eating next winter in burrows under the snow. Once we sat watching the runways of a colony of Hay Mice. Quick as a snake's tongue, the little rodents darted across from one burrow opening to another. We set pit-fall traps by sinking cans across their runways.

I searched constantly—in vain—for snail samples, but I did find some gray round segmented worms or larvae in the water under the rocks.* In the sand and mud of the stream, there were also many smaller worms which

---

*We did not know at this time of the high pesticide residue carried by these hawks. This poses the greatest danger. Of all the bird specimens tested, the Rough-leg specimen had the highest content.

*These worms had the highest pesticide content of all samples tested.

served as an abundant food supply for the tattlers and sandpipers.

*   *   *

The mosquitoes we had been dreading never did materialize in exorbitant numbers—not enough to be a real nuisance. We didn't use the mosquito-netting "tent" I had sewed, except to keep flies off the drying specimens. Neither did we use the head nets. We wore mosquito-proof clothing and used repellents on our hands and faces for the brief period in July when mosquitoes appeared, then we were bothered no more.

Mosquitoes are mainly a psychological problem. Prepare for them, then learn to ignore their buzzing. We learned that when we were tired the high-pitched humming annoyed us, but not otherwise. Like the Arctic wolf, these insects serve their purpose in the chain of life. Mosquitoes furnish abundant food supply for the birds which migrate here to raise their young.

It was interesting to watch the speedy development of Precious, the young Arctic Tern. When seventeen days old he stretched his long narrow wings and flew a few feet. Two days later he flew around in circles overhead for about a two-hundred-foot flight before settling down on the same rocky spit where he could usually be found. He looked much like an adult, except for shorter wings and tail, and he did not yet have a full black cap. His beak and legs were still pink. It was not long before he was flying around with his parents, softly whispering "chi-chi-chi-chi," practicing for the long voyage ahead.

When the Mew Gulls brought their youngsters to our end of the lake, we were surprised they had twins, all gray and as alike as two peas in a pod. We compared

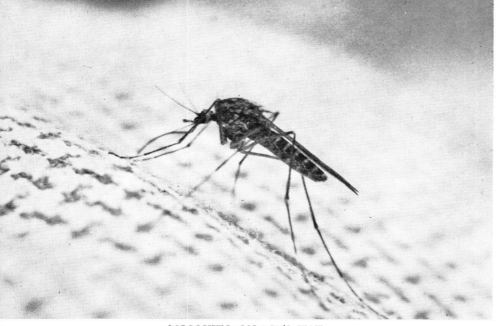

MOSQUITO ON VIV'S HAT
Mosquitoes are mainly a psychological problem. Prepare for them, then learn
to ignore their buzzing.

their progress to that of the precocious Precious. We saw
the juvenal tern flying giddily back and forth, in sheer
exuberance, just playing. The gulls learned to fly about
the same time, but they were clumsy in comparison.
Precious played with the gull chicks, flying rings around
them in intricate aerial acrobatics.

The dusty-gray gull chicks (we called them the "Gull-
dust Twins") were inseparable, swimming or resting side
by side, or flying together. Their devoted parents were
constantly in attendance, stuffing them with fish, trying
to satisfy their insatiable appetites. One day, we noticed
the male parent was gone. He probably got fed up with
the way his progeny mobbed him every time he brought
them food. After a three-day absence, the father gull
made an appearance again. The gull chicks flew around
him excitedly, mewing loudly, as if to say, "Goody,

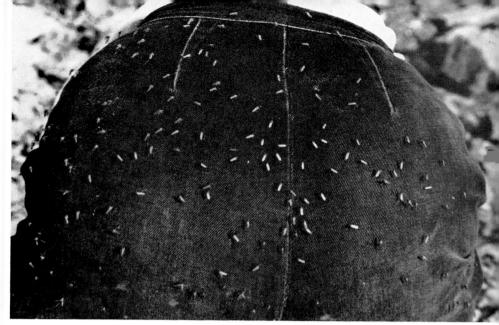

MOSQUITOES

We wore mosquito-proof clothing and used repellents on our hands and faces for the brief period they were a problem. Mosquitoes serve their purpose in the chain of life—they furnish an abundant supply of food for the birds.

goody, Daddy's home." Mother Gull joined in welcoming him. But Daddy did not stay. His boisterous, clamoring offspring were too much for him. He took off and we didn't see him again.

On the eighth of August, an unusually strong cold north wind presaged the beginning of winter. Seeking refuge from the unpleasant wind, Gil and I hiked south below the rim of the lake, where Gil indulged in a little fishing. When we returned to camp, the terns were no longer with us. Taking advantage of a favorable wind, they had started on their incredible journey to the opposite end of the earth—to join the Penguins in the Antarctic.

We missed the terns. How empty the sky overhead seemed without them. We wondered which route they would take. Would it be along the Pacific Coast, or would they fly the circuitous ancestral route across the top of Canada, then the North Atlantic to the west coast of Africa, following it to the South Atlantic? Or would they join those of the species that cross the Atlantic again near the equator to follow the east coast of South America, thence to Antarctica? Our hearts went with them, especially the fun-loving young tern, who was the product of the longest and most hazardous migration—and weeks of tender care.

When we went to bed that night, it was a bone-chilling 36 degrees, with the strong north wind continuing.

Numbers of Water Pipits had been migrating through the valley. Now we saw they were all over the slopes and realized the magnitude of the pipit migration. Supposedly moving from regions farther north, they were abundant at the high and low elevations. We considered them the most abundant species the last part of July.

We missed the fervent songs, color and hustle-bustle

ON THE EIGHTH OF AUGUST, AN UNUSUALLY STRONG, COLD
NORTH WIND PRESAGED THE BEGINNING OF WINTER

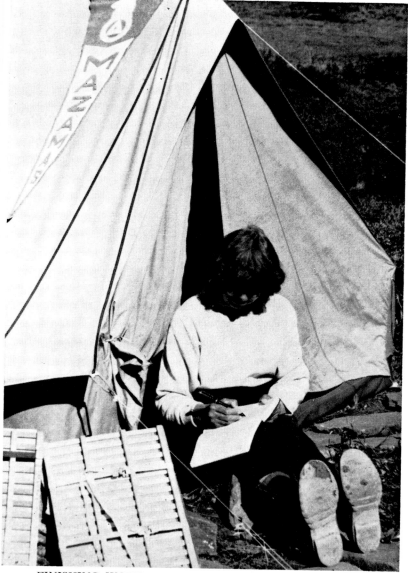

FINISHING WORK ON RECORDS IN PREPARATION FOR
LEAVING LOON LAKE
Plant presses on the left

of the nesting activities, but the excitement of the migrations, real and pending, was contagious. Six or eight Redpolls got carried away and impetuously joined some Water Pipits heading south, excitedly chirping in their undulating flight. Then seeming to have second thoughts, they returned to stay a while longer. The time was approaching when we too would be on our way south. After a summer of continuous daylight, we wondered what it would be like to experience darkness again. How would it feel to again join our own species? We clung to the last hours of wilderness living, savoring the quiet peace and association with the wild ones.

It was time we were leaving. Our shoepacs were wearing out. After hiking a total of six hundred miles, measured by Gil's pedometer, my boots were leaking and Gil's were thin. Gil had patched them repeatedly with surgical tape to extend their service to the end.

We packaged the plant and pesticide specimens and watched our wildlife neighbors—those which still remained.

Weather was beautiful August tenth when we began getting ready to leave Loon Lake. Andy was due to pick us up the following day. After breakfast, we spent several hours cleaning up the camping area. We picked up every vestige of debris we had left—even little bits of metal foil and "twist-em" bands. Burnable material was piled on the bare rocks of the shore. All tin cans (most containers were plastic) were opened with our "G.I." can opener, flattened and placed in our largest tin container —a fifty-pound shortening canister—along with the cardboard and other flammable material. Then all was burned. When we were finished, there was no paint left

VIV'S WORN-OUT SHOEPACS AFTER SIX HUNDRED MILES
OF HIKING ON THE TUNDRA IN ONE SUMMER

on the tins and the large container was about one-third filled.

Not wanting to leave the "incinerator" for the bears to scatter, we hoped to sink it in the deepest water of the lake. We wired a lid on securely and punched a few small holes in the bottom of the can. Since the wind was from the northwest, we carried our condensed package of burned tins a hundred yards west of camp and set it adrift on the lake. The wind began to carry the container of refuse as it sank slowly. Ten minutes later, with a great feeling of satisfaction, we saw it sink out of sight forever.

The morning of the day that Andy was to come for us was cool and cloudy. Gil rose early and fried the last of our canned bacon, serving it with powdered eggs.

We expected our bushpilot about noon and hurried to finish packing our gear and supplies. While we were working, a male ptarmigan stayed near camp. We saw the three tattler chicks foraging on shore. Baird's Sandpipers were feeding near the inlet. Five male Harlequins floated together on the lake. We hated to say goodbye to this wild community, but many of the birds would soon be on their way too.

Gil took our tent down. The campsite looked strangely empty without it. By three p.m. we had carried all our possessions about one hundred yards to where the water was deep enough for the float plane to get close to shore. Staying close to our stack of dunnage, we sat waiting for Andy. We didn't dare leave, for he could come at any moment. It stayed cloudy and chilly, with the interminable north wind, so we built a fire to keep warm.

At six o'clock, we hurriedly fixed hot soup, hot chocolate and coffee. Still no Andy!

"I hear a plane!" Gil looked around, excitedly. It was seven p.m.

We scurried around to get the last items together and ran down to the rocky shore, waiting and watching for the plane.

But Gil had been mistaken. There was no plane. The wind continued to blow. We shivered and put on our warmest clothing.

"It's better flying in the evening—less bumpy," Gil explained to me. "Andy likes to fly in the evening."

We executed a few calisthenics to keep warm while we waited.

At 10:30 p.m., we were still sitting on the shore, expecting Andy at any moment. Temperature was 37 degrees.

"Are you sure this is the right day?" Gil turned to me suspiciously.

"Of course! I've checked off every day." Gil started to thumb through my diary to see if I had numbered all the days correctly.

"I hope he didn't crack up. Maybe he forgot us." Gil was listening for a plane motor.

"Oh, no. He would never forget us," I replied confidently.

By eleven p.m., I too was wondering if he had forgotten.

In the chilly wind, we carried the tent, air mattress, and some of our clothes back up to our old campsite. By midnight we were again in our sack in the little Klepper tent beside Loon Lake.

August 12th, we woke up with the feeling that we had been forgotten. Another morning was spent in getting ready to leave, just in case our pilot showed up. Meanwhile we planned to ration food in case we had to spend more time in the wilderness. Gil had the rifle and some ammunition for hunting, so we would not starve.

Some of our gear was stacked by the shore. Some was packed and at camp, while the rest was halfway between. We decided to wait one more day before unpacking and establishing camp again.

While we were waiting, I wanted to give one more try at searching for my prescription colored glasses up on Ursus Peak. After an early lunch, I climbed up about a thousand feet on the rocky slope of the mountain while Gil stayed at camp. The sun was shining. A beautiful day. I enjoyed the exercise of climbing after a day spent sitting down on the shore.

I looked up and down the valley and on the slopes for grizzlies. None was in sight, but I kept glancing all around. They seem to appear when least expected.

Just beginning to search for my glasses, I heard Gil yell. He heard a plane again. I hoped it was real this time. Then I saw a plane splash down on the lake and taxi toward the north end. I raced madly down the mountain.

Gil introduced me to Dick Wein. Andy, he told us, was "out on charter" and not working out of Bettles at the time. No one else knew we were to be picked up. Quite by chance, somebody had flipped back a page on the calendar and noticed "Pick up Staenders" in Andy's handwriting.

"Boy!" I told the pilot, "Am I glad to see you!"

Chapter XVII

"Furthermore, We Like It!"

*How willingly we would escape the
barriers, escape the sophistication . . .
and suffer nature to entrance us.*

IT WAS LATE EVENING, JUNE 23RD, TWO YEARS LATER, WHEN
Gil and I were winging our way north for another summer's stay in the Brooks Range. Gil sat up front with
the pilot, while I sat in back with our stack of dunnage.
Flying low, first over the muskeg, then over winding
Arctic rivers rippling back and forth beneath us like
silvery ribbons, we bounced close to the edges of the
ridges on a bumpy ride back toward Loon Lake. The
heavy-bodied flying boat, called a Widgeon, plunged up
and down, teetering from one side to the other in the
turbulent air currents as if we were on a roller-coaster.
Our unperturbed pilot, the capable Bud Wood, *hoped*
the ice on Loon Lake would be in such a position that
he could put us down.

We recognized Hunt Fork below. Moments later, we
were flying north over the familiar hourglass lake. We
looked down to see ice covering both wide ends of the
lake, with a narrow space of open water in the middle.
Bud banked steeply into a sharp turn south, and we
swung down swiftly to the north end of the lake. We
seemed to float over the ice. I held my breath, waiting
for the splashdown.

We skimmed just above the water, then over the ice at the south end, over the rim, and away from the lake.

"Oh, no!" I thought. "Now we will be going back, have the expense of the flight, and be right back where we started—at the airstrip."

Surprisingly, the plane banked into another about-face. We were heading back to the lake. Gil turned around and grinned at me.

We flew low over the rocky rim, scooted over the ice at the south end, and exactly at the edge, we plunged into the lake. Suddenly, we were streaking through the water like a speedboat. Water sprayed over the windshield, obscuring our vision. As I was forced forward from the force of the deceleration, I saw the lake surface at eye-level on the side windows. We were deep in the water, the ice looming ahead. We came to a splashing, churning halt just before we bumped it.

Later, I asked Bud why he hadn't splashed down on the first run.

"I didn't know if there was enough open water. I was counting seconds as we flew over. I counted eleven seconds. We needed only ten." As soon as the plane was in the water, he had lowered the landing gear for more drag to slow us down. A superb performance.

It was nearing midnight when Gil, in hip boots, piggy-backed me to shore. Then he and Bud unloaded our supplies and waded ashore with them. We were on the east part of the narrow part of the lake. The frowning crags of Ursus towered above.

"Why on earth do you people want to spend a summer in this desolate place?" Our bushpilot looked around at the sterile rockbound shore, the treeless valley, the gray-brown peaks.

WE RETURN TO LOON LAKE TWO YEARS LATER
The bush pilot left us on the east side of the lake. Ice choked the north end

"We have work to do," I replied. "Furthermore, we like it!"

Bud shook his head, a puzzled expression on his face.

The pesticide samples Gil and I had collected two years before had confirmed the suspicions of the scientists at the Federal Research Center of the United States Wildlife Service at Denver. Insecticidal residues had been found in the samples. Traces in some, considerable amounts in others. D. Glen Crabtree, Chief of Pesticide-Wildlife Studies, wanted duplicate samples so that a comparison could be made. Contamination in the Rough-legged Hawks was high enough to cause concern. If possible, Gil and I were to get samples of the same hawks.

It started raining that midnight just after our bush-pilot left us on the rocky shore of Loon Lake beneath the cliffs of Ursus. We glassed around for grizzlies, then set up our tent, covered our supplies with a tarp, and went to bed. We woke with a start. Rocks were rolling down Ursus. We grabbed our binoculars and went outside to look around, expecting to see a grizzly. Nothing moved. We zipped up the tent and snuggled down again, feeling right at home in the wilderness.

The next day, in a steady rain, we worked at relaying our 650 pounds of dunnage about a mile over sloping wet rocks to the old campsite at the north end of the lake. On one of the relays, I was carrying a heavy load when my rubber-soled shoepacs skidded on the slippery stones. My knee scrunched down on a razor-sharp rock. Excruciating pain made me think my leg was broken. I sat waiting for the pain to ease.

"What a way to start out the summer," I thought, "with

a broken leg." That would really slow me down, and poor Gil would have a lot of extra work to do.

Other than being concerned with the work, I was not worried. Broken bones in the wilderness are not fatal. They will always heal, and if the bones don't heal together properly, they can be rebroken and reset later.

Luckily, my knee was only badly bruised. A half hour later I was working again, with a limp, helping Gil ferry our dunnage the rest of the way to the place where we had camped before.

It was like coming home—except that someone else had visited Loon Lake in the interval. Hunters, probably, had left debris and litter all over the place. There were cardboard cartons, bits of canvas, and papers and plastics strewn over the tundra, along with whiskey bottles and tin cans that had been used for target practice.

Litter in civilization is bad enough, but in the wilderness, it is very sad. Someone has said it is worse than littering a church, because a church at least has a janitor. Muttering between our teeth at the desecration wrought by "civilized" people, we worked many hours to pick up and dispose of the debris.

One of the first things we noticed was that there were fewer birds than two years before. Especially fewer sparrows.

The terns of Tern Peninsula had not made it back this year. We missed them. But there was a pair nesting at the south end territory. The Mew Gulls were nesting *in the same nest*, a shallow scrape at the very top of their peninsula.

Our first objective was to see if the Rough-legged Hawks were still nesting in the old territory. We would try to get a sample for analysis.

From my diary:

We left about 11 a.m. to see if we could find the hawks. Walking was not bad as we headed north. I remarked to Gil that where birds had scolded all along the way two years ago, now there was only one now and then. We began climbing and realized there were no birds on the slope. As we climbed, we went probably one-half mile and no birds at all. We went a mile—still no birds. I felt like crying. Where were they? What had happened to all the Tree Sparrows and White-crowns that had made the slope alive two years before?

We reached a small gorge and used an animal trail to get down into it. It was 12:30 and the clean, cool stream invited us to stop for lunch. As we sat there, a pair of tattlers scolded. They flew downstream, then up and down and up again, scolding. A single Tree Sparrow flew by. We heard a Golden-crown sing his three whistled notes on the mountain slope above us.

The Rough-legs were there in their territory, but using an alternate nest. This aerie would be difficult to reach. We studied the hawk's cliff from the opposite side of the canyon. The aerie was on a sturdy shelf, beneath a forbidding overhang, with no good belay point above it. There would be no safe way to descend directly to it. Below the nest was a chimney at the bottom of which was a narrow ledge leading to the right. If we could get on that ledge! Twenty feet to the right, at the other end of the ledge, was a chimney I thought climbable. We could anchor a belayer at the top of that.

Gil thought it would be too risky to attempt. But we really wanted that hawk sample, and I insisted that I was light enough. He could give me an effective belay. If it became too dangerous, I would retreat. If I got in trouble, he could haul me back up. Gil consented to let me try.

We hiked back to camp to get three steel angle tent stakes for "pitons" to anchor the belay man, some nylon slings, and our best rope—a ⅜-inch nylon line. We would use it doubled. I planned to rappel down the thirty-foot chimney. With an upper belay, I would traverse twenty feet on the narrow ledge to get below the hawk nest. From there I could climb up the twenty feet to the aerie. Our main concern was that the rock was crumbly—what we call "rotten rock."

With the improvised pitons, Gil anchored himself securely at the top of the cliff and prepared to belay me. I tied in, and stepped on a solid-looking rock at the top of the vertical chimney I planned to descend. The rock started slipping. I jumped back just in time. It tumbled over the precipice, hit once, then silently bounced into space. We heard a thunderous crash as it hit the bottom of the canyon.

"Let's give it up," Gil said shakily. "It's too dangerous. This rock is treacherous."

Looking over the edge, we both knew the consequences if either of us should be seriously injured. There would be no help for over two months. And, although we spoke of it only once, always in the back of our minds was the gruesome fact that if either of us was killed the remaining one would be compelled to choose between guarding the body for the rest of the summer or letting it be eaten by grizzlies or wolves. There would be no burial in the permafrost.

I took a deep breath and stepped on another rock at the top of the chimney. I stomped down hard on it. It was solid.

"It's okay. I'll be all right," I assured him. "It's my fault. I should have tested it before I stepped there. I'm ready to descend."

"Belay on! Be careful!"

I slid down the rope easily, careful not to touch any rock which could be loose, until I reached the six-inch-wide ledge which led south under a series of overhanging sharp vertical rock fins for twenty feet to a tiny platform under the nest. Some rocks came loose as I began the delicate traverse. I flipped the light belay line over each vertical razor-sharp fin as I inched carefully along the crumbly narrow ledge.

I remember thinking I was glad my mother didn't know where I was and that Gil could not see my situation. Should I fall, the sharp rocky fins would probably cut my life-line. *I must not fall.* I stopped a few times, debating whether I should risk going on. Then I thought of how important it was to get a sample from the Rough-legs and forced myself to continue. With extreme care, I sidled along the tiny ledge under the protruding fins. At last, I reached the small stance under the hawk nest.

For the moment I was safe enough. I yelled to my climbing partner to let him know. If we could only flip the rope over the last menacing fins without damaging it, Gil could hold me in case I slipped while climbing up the crumbly twenty feet of rock to the aerie. After several attempts, we flipped the rope successfully. I scrabbled for holds, while working up to the nest.

The parent Rough-legs were in great distress. My eyes reached the level of the nest and two downy baby hawks stared at me. Trustingly, one chick crept toward me, opening his beak to be fed. I cuddled it for awhile. Then I found and collected two unhatched eggs before going back down to the small stance below and making the tricky traverse back over the narrow ledge.

✿   ✿   ✿

GIL AT HUNT FORK
With rain chaps tied at the bottom and used as waders on our second visit
to tree line.

July 19th, we trekked down to Hunt Fork and found the Rough-legs were nesting there again. Gil held the line while I made a perfectly safe descent to the ledge where the nest was. I startled the three downy young. One flipped over on his back, defensively. I was shocked to see the poor little thing hanging head-down over the edge of the nest, ready to slide over the face of the cliff. He started to slip, but I saw that his talons gripped a couple of sticks in the nest, keeping him from sliding farther. An egg was caught on some sticks at the extreme outer edge of the nest, below the frightened chick.

I wondered how to get the egg without further frightening the chick into letting go of his precarious grip. The hawklet eyed me while I eyed the egg. With extreme care, I moved slowly, reaching my hand out beside the chick until I clasped the egg. I retreated just as cautiously, avoiding any fast move. The baby hawk was still regarding me suspiciously, still on his back, hanging on for dear life to keep from sliding out of the nest. I wanted to place it safely back in the nest but didn't dare touch it for fear it would let go and plunge down into the canyon.

A few days later, on our way back to Loon Lake, we flushed an eagle from a huge stick nest. It flew up and away with an angry cry. From the cliff above, we tried to look into the nest, but an overhang blocked our view. We had no rope with us at the time.

"I'll stretch out on the ground behind you and hang onto your legs while you try to look in," Gil offered.

He lay prostrate on the sloping top of the cliff, hanging onto my ankles, as we both inched down and forward, like children playing "choo-choo train," until I was hanging in space over the precipice. The nest was empty. Large sticks identified it as an eagle's aerie, but there were no green branches—proof that it was not being used. In good repair, it had probably been used the year before and was now an alternate nest.

✧ ✧ ✧

Shortly before we were due to be picked up by our bush pilot in August, we backpacked to a high lake on the south side of Loon Peak. Smooth as glass, protected from the winds on all sides, the placid lake mirrored the craggy ridges of Loon. We called it "Serene." We camped there at Serene Lake beside a delightful brook where sparkling water swirled and gurgled around bright orange and cream lichen-covered rocks.

On our return to base camp, we found that a party of four hunters had been flown in. Their tent was pitched close to ours and they had already been up on the slopes looking for trophies. The sheep, which had been getting ever closer to camp, suddenly vanished.

One of the hunters reported a caribou carcass near the summit of Ursus. Gil and I wanted a pesticide sample from it. When we started out after eight in the evening to climb Ursus, it was raining. Up on the high ridges, with clouds hanging dark and gloomy, it was snowing. We climbed into the storm.

Once again Gil and I found ourselves on the summit of Ursus at midnight. Close to the middle of August, at the darkest hour of the twenty-four, under a heavy blanket of storm clouds, it was snowing heavily. We walked around in a blurry blizzard, looking for a caribou carcass. At first, when the snow was only a few inches deep, we saw vague outlines of dark rocks, but the snow continued to pile up steadily.

"Let's give up," Gil suggested. "We couldn't find a caribou carcass in this storm."

"Let's go on," I begged. "I know just exactly where he said it is lying."

We wandered around in the snowstorm, in half-light, trying to recognize the features of the mountain.

"Let's go back, before we get lost." Gil stopped.

"It's not much farther," I insisted. "Just over that low ridge there."

We proceeded a little farther. The mountain top looked different in the storm. Gil again stopped dead in his tracks.

"We're not going any farther. That carcass, covered with snow, could be less than twenty feet away and we wouldn't know it. I'm not going one step farther."

"You're not?" I feigned surprise. "You wait here. I want to go over to that embankment." I thought I recognized it. "I'll be back shortly."

"Don't go," Gil warned.

"I'll be back in a few minutes. It won't take long." I started out, trying to identify vague shapes in the dim light.

Gil followed a short distance, then refused to budge. "We have no compass. We might get turned around and have to walk many miles if we come down on the wrong side of the mountain."

Stubbornly, I kept going, sure that I could find the carcass in a few minutes. Finally, peering into the gloom, I decided I should return to Gil. I could just vaguely see his dark form in the murky distance.

We found our way down the mountain and returned to camp without our pesticide sample.

The next morning, we told the hunter, an oceanog-

ON LOON PEAK
Lover's Gully, leading up Ursus Peak, in background

rapher, about our failure to find the carcass. He was going in that direction, he said, to carry out the remainder of a sheep he had shot. He would get the samples for us. In better light, although it was still snowing, he climbed Ursus. Not until he was less than one hundred feet from it did he see the carcass—with a huge blond grizzly on top of it. The bear stood up on his hind legs, facing the man, and growled his resentment. He was playing "finders-keepers." The hunter backed away, wisely deciding not to contest the bear's right to his find.

After each had shot his sheep, the hunters were anxious to leave with their meat and trophies. The bush-pilot came in and took them away, and Gil and I were alone with the wildlife once more. A few days later, the sheep began to appear on the cliffs again. They knew who their friends were!

When the time came to bid our second farewell, we

VIV ON SUMMIT OF LOON PEAK
Hunt Fork River in the distance. Overflow ice to the left of center, ten miles away.

really hated to leave. An intangible something about
the untamed land and wildlife of the Arctic had taken
hold of us. As Emerson has said, "Nature satisfies by its
loveliness. . . . In the wilderness, [we] find something
more dear and connate."

FLYING OVER THE ENDICOTT MOUNTAINS, BROOKS RANGE

Flying home after a summer in the Arctic

APPENDIX

Tribute to Rachel Carson

Rachel Carson, a courageous and perceptive scientist, published *Silent Spring* in 1962. Immediately there was a hue and cry from the petro-chemical companies trying to discredit the instant best seller. Today, there is not a biologist or ecologist who is not alarmed at the degree of pollution in the entire world by synthetic chemicals—especially chlorinated hydrocarbons.

Miss Carson was a biologist who studied genetics in her graduate work at Johns Hopkins University. From 1936 to 1952, she served as a staff biologist and editor for the United States Fish and Wildlife Service. On resigning from government service, she was awarded the Department of Interior's Distinguished Service Award.

Other honors accorded Miss Carson: the Gold Medal of the New York Zoological Society, the John Burroughs Medal, the Gold Medal of the Geographical Society of Philadelphia, the National Book Award for non-fiction (*The Sea Around Us*). Under a Guggenheim Fellowship, she studied offshore life and then wrote *The Edge of the Sea.*

In all her work, Rachel Carson's basic interest has been the relation of life to its environment. She collected data from scientists all over the world about the long-term effects of deadly chemicals, especially synthetic insecticides, on the living community. The result was *Silent Spring*—a courageous revelation of the forces that mod-

ern man has brought into being in his ruthless war on
nature, an eloquent protest in behalf of the unity of all
nature, *a protest in behalf of life.*

Appendix B

List of Pesticides Found in Samples

A REPORT BY THE UNITED STATES FISH AND WILDLIFE SERVICE

From D. Glen Crabtree, Chief, Section of Chemical, Physiological and Pesticide-Wildlife Studies, Denver Wildlife Research Center, Denver, Colorado. Analytical results of Brooks Range, Alaska, samples collected by the Staenders—summer 1964.

Specimens were scrutinized very closely by gas, thin-layer and paper chromatography. In the case of the former, two different columns were employed to differentiate the various compounds found.

TABLE OF PESTICIDE FINDINGS

Invoice No.	Description of Sample	Staender Sample No.	Insecticide Found	Amount found in ppm. (parts per million)
6386	Rodent (Tundra Vole)	50	DDE	0.4
			p,p'DDT	0.3
6387	Round Segmented worms or larvae	44	DDE	3.3
			p,p'DDT	1.8
6388	Composite of five Sculpin	41		
		42	DDE	0.1
		43	DDD	Trace*
		45		
		46		
6389	Arctic Char	19	DDE	Trace
6390	Arctic Char	34	DDE	Trace
6391	Grayling	38	DDE	Trace
6392	Grayling	18	DDE	Trace
6394	Arctic Char	37	DDE	0.1
6395	Tundra Vole	47	DDE	0.1
6396	Singing Vole	49	DDE	0.2
6397	Tundra Vole	98	DDE	Trace
6398	Lemming	35	DDE	0.7
			p,p'DDT	0.4
6408	Gray-cheeked Thrush	14	DDE	0.6
6409	Two young from Eastern Robin nest	8	DDE	0.8
6410	Composite of eggs from 3 nests:			
	Yellow Wagtail	5		
	Gray-cheeked Thrush	10	DDE	0.3
	Common Redpoll	15		
6411	Common Redpoll (3 young)	7	DDE	0.9
6412	Rough-legged Hawk egg	13	DDE	2.4
			DDD	0.9
			p,p'DDT	0.1
6413	Harlequin duckling	9(c)	DDE	0.1
6496	Composite of eggs from 3 nests:			
	Horned Lark	1		
	Savannah Sparrow	3	DDE	0.3
	Lapland Longspur	4		
6497	Composite of eggs from 4 nests:			
	Gambel's White-crowned Sparrow	2	DDE	1.8
	Tree Sparrow	11	p,p'DDT	Trace
	Eastern Tree Sparrow	16		
	Gambel's White-crowned Sparrow	30		
6498	Harlequin duck egg	9(b)	DDE	0.3
			DDD	0.8

*Trace=Less than 0.1 ppm.

In addition to the above samples twelve vegetative samples were collected and analyzed but no residues of insecticides were found in measurable amounts, although a group of contaminates were present in all samples in about the same amount. So far these compounds have been unidentifiable and may have obscured traces of pesticides in these samples.

Commercial grades of DDT will sometimes contain a small percentage of DDD, but it has been established that DDD and DDE are, or can be, metabolites of DDT. The compound o,p'DDT is a less active isomer of the ordinary p,p'DDT. In the words of the layman, DDT does not remain as DDT, but changes or metabolizes to DDD, DDE and other compounds until it finally degrades to DDA when (in animals) it is eliminated in the urine.

Abbreviations: DDT—1,1,1-trichloro-2,2-bis(p-chlorophenyl)ethane;
DDE—1,1-dichloro-2,2-bis(p-chlorophenyl)ethylene;
DDD—1,1-dichloro-2,2-bis(p-chlorophenyl)ethane;
DDA—bis(p-chlorophenyl)acetic acid.

It is interesting to note that the worms (Inv. No. 6387), which were found in a stream under a rock, contained a high concentration of the pesticides. The very high contamination in the Rough-legged Hawk egg puts the hawks' survival in real danger. The eggs in Samples No. 11, 16, and 30 (Inv. No. 6497) had been incubated but did not hatch. The Harlequin duck egg (Inv. 6498) had been incubated but was sterile (high concentration of contamination) but its nest-mate Harlequin duckling (Inv. 6413), had a lesser amount and developed but died in the shell. The two young robins (Inc. 6409) also had a high amount and were found dead under the nest with two live young still in the nest.

All of the bird samples were eggs or young, therefore the contamination was passed on to the young from the parents and/or environment. The birds could get some contamination through migration, but all of the rodents tested had measurable insecticide contamination—some in considerable amounts. We were informed that the fish (except the Sculpins) migrate downstream in the fall and return upstream in the spring.

Some Shocking Facts

We should outlaw the use of certain highly destructive pesticides such as DDT, Dieldrin, Aldrin, Heptachlor, Endrin, Lindane, Chlordane, and other "hard," or persistent chemicals used to kill insects. Our environment is now so polluted that we can no longer eat any food or drink any fluid without swallowing minute amounts of these chemicals. DDT is found in the Antarctic Ocean, thousands of miles from where pesticides have been applied. We have found it in the Arctic in worms under rocks in the streams. It is found in the fish life of deep oceans and inside the eggs of all birds of prey—eggs which do not hatch into birds whose numbers are now in decline. We kill songbirds and prevent the birth of Bald Eagles, our national symbol, with these pesticides.

Two years ago, a United States Public Health Service study showed that the average American has gathered 12 parts per million of DDT into his human fatty tissue, as well as .15 of a part per million of Dieldrin. Nursing mothers now impart .08 of a part per million of DDT in human milk given their infants. No one yet knows what 12 parts per million in human fatty tissue means, except that it will stay there. This is beyond the standard set by the United States Department of Agriculture for our own food. DDT in far smaller concentrations has awesome consequences for many small or simple forms of animal life. What it means for human life is not yet known.

DDT is even found in the rain. One study shows that up to half of all DDT spread by airplanes does not settle but escapes into the atmosphere to circle the globe.

The United States Department of Interior no longer allows the use of these dangerous chemicals on federal lands, except under certain isolated and restricted conditions. Yet anyone can go to the local garden shop and buy them in gallon lots to use on a farm or garden.

A. L. Roberts, D.V.M., Canyon Pet Hospital, Portland, Oregon, reports a number of cats and dogs are suffering and dying from damage to central nervous systems (brain and spinal cord) and kidney and liver damage because of flea collars and running on gardens sprayed with chlorinated hydrocarbons.

Dr. M. Jacqueline Verrett, from F.D.A.'s Bureau of Science, has been investigating effects of the fungicides captan, folpet and related chemicals on developing chicken embryos. She found they caused birth deformities in chickens. These fungicides have the same chemical structure as thalidomide, which caused birth deformities in humans. The above chemicals have not been tested on humans.

New, safe insecticides are on the market. More are being developed. There is now no excuse for using the dangerous ones.

One final note of warning. Be extremely careful of disposing of jugs of the hard pesticides which have gathered dust in your garden shed. Do not put them in your garbage can or flush them down the sewer system. Call your local Environmental Council, if you have one. If no other way is found, bury them very deeply—in glass containers—where they are certain not to be disturbed.

—Lake Oswego, Oregon, June 1969

Birds Identified at Loon Lake

COMMON LOON, *Gavia immer.*
ARCTIC LOON, *Gavia arctica.*
RED-THROATED LOON, *Gavia stellata.*
CANADA GOOSE, *Branta canadensis.*
GREEN-WINGED TEAL, *Anas carolinensis.* (D.Y.)
AMERICAN WIDGEON, *Mareca americana.*
GREATER SCAUP, *Aythya marila.**
OLDSQUAW, *Clangula hyemalis.* (D.Y.)
HARLEQUIN DUCK, *Histrionicus histrionicus.**
SURF SCOTER, *Melanitta perspicillata.*
RED-BREASTED MERGANSER, *Mergus serrator.*
ROUGH-LEGGED HAWK, *Buteo lagapus.**
GOLDEN EAGLE, *Aquila chrysaetos.*
GYRFALCON, *Falco rusticolus.*
PIGEON HAWK, *Falco columbarius.*
ROCK PTARMIGAN, *Lagopus mutus.* (D.Y.)
AMERICAN GOLDEN PLOVER, *Pluvialis dominica.**
COMMON SNIPE, *Capella gallinago.*
UPLAND PLOVER, *Bartramia longicauda.*
SPOTTED SANDPIPER, *Actitis macularia.*
WANDERING TATTLER, *Peteroscelus incannum.**
BAIRD'S SANDPIPER, *Erolia bairdii.**
LEAST SANDPIPER, *Erolia mimutilla.* (D.Y.)

(Asterisk signifies nest record for species. D.Y. is for Downy Young, F. Y. means Fledged Young observed)

SEMIPALMATED SANDPIPER, *Ereunetes pusillus.* (D.Y.)

WESTERN SANDPIPER, *Ereunetes mauri.* (D.Y.)

NORTHERN PHALAROPE, *Lobipes lobatus.**

LONG-TAILED JAEGER, *Stercorarius longicaudus.**

GLAUCOUS GULL, *Larus hyperboreau.*

MEW GULL, *Larus canus.**

ARCTIC TERN, *Sterna paradisaea.**

SHORT-EARED OWL, *Asio flammeus.*

YELLOW-SHAFTED FLICKER, *Colaptes auratus.**

SAY'S PHOEBE, *Sayornis saya.**

HORNED LARK, *Eremophila alpestris.**

VIOLET-GREEN SWALLOW, *Tachycineta thalassina.**

GRAY JAY, *Perisoreus canadensis.* (F.Y.)

COMMON RAVEN, *Corvus corax.**

BOREAL CHICKADEE, *Parus hudsonicus.* (F.Y.)

GRAY-HEADED CHICKADEE, *Parus cinctus.* (F.Y.)

DIPPER, *Cinclus mexicanus.*

ROBIN, *Turdus migratorius.**

VARIED THRUSH, *Ixoreus naevius.* (F.Y.)

GRAY-CHEEKED THRUSH, *Hylocichla minima.**

WHEATEAR, *Oenanthe oenanthe.**

TOWNSEND'S SOLITAIRE, *Myadestes townsendi.* (F.Y.)

ARCTIC WARBLER, *Phylloscopus borealis.**

RUBY-CROWNED KINGLET, *Regulus calendula.*

YELLOW WAGTAIL, *Motacilla flava.**

WATER PIPIT, *Anthus spinoletta.**

NORTHERN SHRIKE, *Lanius excubitor.**

MYRTLE WARBLER, *Dendroica coronata.* (F.Y.)

———

(Asterisk signifies nest record for species. D.Y. is for Downy Young, F. Y. means Fledged Young observed)

WILSON'S WARBLER, *Wilsonia pusilla.**

GRAY-CROWNED ROSY FINCH, *Leucosticte tephrocotis.**

REDPOLL, *Acanthis.**

SAVANNAH SPARROW, *Passerculus sandwichensis.**

SLATE-COLORED JUNCO, *Junco hyemalis.* (F.Y.)

TREE SPARROW, *Spizella arborea.**

GAMBEL'S WHITE-CROWNED SPARROW, *Zonotrichia leucophrys gambelii.**

GOLDEN-CROWNED SPARROW, *Zonotrichia atricapilla.**

FOX SPARROW, *Passerella iliaca.**

LAPLAND LONGSPUR, *Calcarius lapponicus.**

SNOW BUNTING, *Plectrophenax nivalis.**

————

(Asterisk signifies nest record for species. D.Y. is for Downy Young, F. Y. means Fledged Young observed)

Temperature Chart and Weather, Summer 1966

(Recording thermometer read at 6 p.m.)

		Lo	Hi	
June	28—	35°	67°	Beautiful. S. wind, 4-16 m.p.h.
	29—	42	72	Windy in a.m., calm in p.m.—scattered showers.
	30—	44	70	Mild, S. wind. Cloudy. Calm in evening.
July	1—	41	75	Hot, windy. Rain in evening—twister blew down shelter.
	2—	46	63	Cool all day. Rain. Strong south wind.
	3—	40	69	Heavy rain in p.m.
	4—	40	69	Nice a.m., cloudy in p.m. Rain from 8 p.m. on. S. wind.
	5—	46	57	Cloudy, S. wind. Rain in a.m.
	6—	45	57	Cloudy, rain. S. wind.
	7—	45	59	Cloudy, scattered showers. S. wind.
	8—	43	60	Cloudy a.m., rain p.m. Nice eve. (left for Hunt Fork)
	9—			(Hunt Fork) Rain.
	10—			(Hunt Fork) Rain.
	11—			(Hunt Fork) Rain.

Lo	Hi	
12—47	54	Very heavy rain.
13—43	50	Heavy rain, S.W. wind.
14—41	69	Beautiful day, calm.
15—41	71	Cloudy p.m., but nice. Mild S. wind.
16—46	56	Cloudy a.m., rain in p.m. S. wind, 10-15 m.p.h.
17—44	51	Cloudy. Rain in eve. S.W. wind, 15-20 m.p.h.
18—41	57	Clearing. Little rain. Mild N. wind.
19—33	69	Beautiful, clear. Coating of ice on bushes. S. and N. wind.
20—37	70	Perfect day. S. wind.
21—51	67	Cloudy, warm. Very little rain. Many mosquitoes.
22—42	69	Cloudy, warm. Gentle S. wind.
23—42	67	Cloudy. S. then N. wind. Few sprinkles.
24—50	72	Cloudy. Warm. Mild S. then N. wind.
25—47	68	Perfect day. N. wind.
26—40	62	Clear. Strong N. wind.
27—40	65	Clear. Cool N. wind. Nice day.
28—40	72	Clear, warm. Wonderful day.
29—35	65	Cloudy. Nice day.
30—37		(Hiked to Serene Lake) Thunder storm.
31—	72	(Returned to base camp) Scattered showers. Hot hiking.

	Lo	Hi	
Aug.	1—47	55	Rain. Snow on peaks. N. then S. wind.
	2—36	55	Cloudy. Little rain. S. wind.
	3—43	54	Cloudy, then rain. S. wind.
	4—41	52	Cloudy, foggy, rain. S. wind. Clearing in evening.
	5—37	66	Cloudy, nice day. S. then N. wind. Clearing in evening.
	6—44	73	Hot. Smoky (from forest fire?) N. then S. wind. 58° at 8:30 p.m.
	7—49	80	Hot. N. wind in evening. Calm most of day.
	8—44	62	Clear. N. wind, 10-20 m.p.h.
	9—36	55	Strong N. wind. Clear.
	10—33	59	Clear. Strong N. wind.
	11—29	66	Freeze. Beautiful day. Moderate N. wind.
	12—32		(Flew out of wilderness).

REMARKS ON SUMMER WEATHER AT LOON LAKE

High temperature readings can be misleading. Weather was subject to sudden changes. We could be suffering from the heat while hiking, then an hour or two later be huddled against a cold wind, in heavy winter clothing.

Since Loon Lake is situated in a deep, narrow north-south valley, the sun went behind Loon Peak around 4 p.m. Then it usually cooled down quickly. Most of the time, the wind situation determined whether we were comfortable or not.

We consider the weather at Loon Lake comparable to winter near Portland, Oregon, or to the summer climate at the summit of Mt. Hood. One can be sun-bathing in sublime weather one moment and a half-hour later be blasted by a cold wind.

Food List for Three Months in Wilderness

10 lbs. Flour
15 lbs. Krusteaz Pancake Mix
 1 lb. Swedish Pancake Mix
13 lbs. Biscuit Mix
2½ lbs. Quaker Oats
2½ lbs. Wheathearts
 1 lb. Wheat Germ
2½ lbs. Familia (3 pkgs.)
3½ lbs. Shredded Wheat
25 lbs. Sugar
 5 lbs. Brown Sugar
 2 lbs. Brownie Mix
 1 lb. Date Bar Mix
12 oz. Macaroon Mix
 6 oz. Baking Powder
 8 oz. Soda
 6 oz. Dry Yeast (21 pkgs. coolrise)
 2 oz. Makasyrup
 3 oz. Spices (nutmeg, cinnamon, Beau Monde)
3¼ lbs. Knorr Soup Mix (28 pkgs.)
12 oz. Red Kettle Soup (6 tins)
 8 oz. Prime Broth Mix (35 pkgs.)
 2 lbs. Assorted Sauce Mixes (19 pkgs.)
28 lbs. Dry Milk (140 qts.)

4 lbs. Swiss Miss
2½ lbs. Coffeemate (3 jars)
13 oz. Powdered Egg
15 oz. Borden's Instant Omelet (8 pkgs.)
6 lbs. Vegetable shortening
21 lbs. Margarine
2 lbs. Jam and Jelly
2 lbs. Honey
2½ lbs. Salt
3½ lbs. Instant Coffee
8 oz. Instant Tea
8 oz. Cocoa
8 lbs. Bacon (8 tins)
6 lbs. Canadian Bacon (3 tins)
6 lbs. Ham (3 tins)
10 lbs. Prem (12 tins)
48 oz. Danish Hard Salami (4 tins)
6 lbs. Meat Balls (6 tins)
1 lb. Kipper Snacks (2 tins)
13 oz. Kipper Snacks (4 tins)
78 oz. Tuna (12 tins)
25 oz. Vienna Sausage (5 tins)
5 oz. Dried Beef
8 lbs. Beef Stick (2 pkgs.)
4 lbs. Tillamook Cheese
22 oz. Quick Rice
4 lbs. Long Grain Rice
6 lbs. Pinto Beans
1 lb. Baby Limas
4 lbs. Macaroni
2 lbs. Frillets
10 oz. Spaghetti
4½ lbs. Instant Yams

1 lb. Dried Cubed Potatoes
6 lbs. Dried Mashed Potatoes (No. 10 tin)
1 lb. Potato Pancake Mix (5 pkgs.)
2½ lbs. Potato Dumpling Mix (5 pkgs.)
18 oz. Freeze-Dried Corn (No. 10 tin)
2 lbs. Split Peas
12 oz. Vegetable Soup Blend (6 pkgs.)
6 oz. Green Pepper Flakes
6 oz. Onion Flakes
3 oz. Celery Flakes
2 lbs. Assorted Dri-lite Vegetables (for backpacking)
8 lbs. Raisins
4 lbs. Figs
3 lbs. Prunes
1 lb. Dates
3 lbs. Vacuum Dried Peaches (No. 10 tin)
2 lbs. Logan Bread
2 lbs. Pilot Bread
20 oz. Triscuit (2 pkgs.)
10 oz. Wheat Thins
11 oz. Sesame Cheese Crackers
10 oz. Rolled Wheat Wafers
3 lbs. Sugar Cookies (Homemade)
6 lbs. Brown Bread (6 tins)
8 oz. Date Nut Roll (1 tin)
39 oz. Cherry and Berry Jello (13 pkgs.)
15 oz. Lime Jello (5 pkgs.)
30 oz. Orange Jello (10 pkgs.)
3 oz. Salad Jello (1 pkg.)
66 oz. Royal Pudding (12 large pkgs.)
39 oz. Whip N'Chill (12 pkgs.)
8 oz. Dream Whip (4 pkgs.)
11 oz. Cheese Cake Pie (1 pkg.)

14 oz. Graham Cracker Crumbs (1 pkg.)
18 oz. Lemonade Mix (6 pkgs.)
 2 oz. Pure Lemon Crystals
38 oz. Start (8 pkgs.)
14 oz. Instant Eggnog (1 pkg.)
 4 lbs. Assorted Toffees
60 oz. Hershey Chocolate (6 bars)
39 oz. Baby Ruth (12 small bars)
36 oz. Licorice
20 oz. Marshmallows
14 oz. Coconut
16 oz. Peanut Brittle
 1 lb. Walnuts (fresh)
 1 lb. Filberts (Roasted)
41 oz. Planters Mixed Nuts (3 tins)

Total weight, with packaging, 310 lbs.

FOOD PACKAGING HINTS

To save weight and space, most foods were repackaged in a way that would be convenient to find and use. As much metal as possible was eliminated. Most packaging was in plastics—bags, jugs, square containers—which were lightweight, rainproof and disposable.

Our largest food bin was a lightweight twenty-gallon metal garbage can. In this we stored flour products, breakfast food and package mixes—all in durable plastic bags. Vertical cardboards formed compartments, which kept flour products, breakfast foods, and mixes separated.

A lightweight metal fifty-pound shortening can was

our Vegetable Bin, with all vegetables, including macaroni products, in plastic bags.

We had four square five-gallon cans which contained fruit, candy and nuts, desserts and beverages, and milk. Extra milk was stored at the bottom of the large bin. All Jello and Start crystals were removed from original packages and poured into wide-mouthed plastic bottles, then measured as used. (The first year we had a mess when water leaked into the bin.)

A separate tin was for crackers and cookies.

Meat and fish, except Beefstick, remained sealed in tins to prevent spoilage. These tins were stored in cardboard cartons and opened one at a time as used.

All margarine was repackaged in three-pound shortening cans lined with plastic bags to prevent the cans from rusting. These were stored as close to the permafrost as possible.

Tea, coffee, salt and miscellanous items were in plastic jugs stored in cardboard cartons or a large duffel bag. Sugar was in three plastic laundry bleach jugs, which were later used as water jugs. Cut in half, they could also be used for mixing bowls. We used the top for a funnel.

A piece of plywood on top of our "garbage can" bin provided an eating table. Two smaller boards on five-gallon cans were our chairs.

Although Gil was the cook, Vivian was in charge of organization. Whatever was needed could be found in a few moments.

Supply List for Three Months in Wilderness

24 lb.	Klepper Tent with poles
1 lb., 6 oz.	Tent pegs
8 lb., 8 oz.	Backpacking tent, poles
4 lb., 12 oz.	Mosquito tent
3 lb.	Clear plastic (12'x15')
2 lb.	Nylon tarp
5 lb.	Ponchos (two)
5 lb.	Ropes and lines
5 lb.	Plywood (4 pieces)
11 lb.	Air mattress
5 lb., 4 oz.	Sleeping bag
6 lb., 10 oz.	Kelty Packs (two)
2 lb., 4 oz.	Climbing packs (two)
2 lb., 8 oz.	Duffel bag
6 lb., 12 oz.	Two Blankets
1 lb., 4 oz.	Hatchet
4 lb., 8 oz.	Coleman stove (single burner) and cook pots
12 oz.	Big cook pot
7 oz.	Wind screen for cooker
1 lb., 11 oz.	Fry pan
4 oz.	Pie plates (metal foil)
1 lb., 10 oz.	Reflector oven
2 lb.	Plastic tub and bowls

     10 oz. Sifter, beater, measuring cup
1 lb., 12 oz. Dishes, eating utensils
5 lb., 6 oz. Scope, with case
2 lb., 7 oz. Binoculars (two)
20 lb.   Cameras and accessories
 7 lb., 4 oz. Tripods (two)
10 lb., 4 oz. Rifle and case (Big Bertha)
5 lb., 12 oz. Ammo, cleaning oils, etc.
2 lb., 7 oz. Ice axe (Viv's)
      4 oz. Pliers
      4 oz. Flare
      6 oz. Wire
1 lb.   Small nails
      9 oz. Clothes pins (2 doz.)
2 lb., 12 oz. Soap (12 bars)
5 lb., 6 oz. Tissue
     12 oz. Head nets, other netting
      4 oz. Mazama flag
40 lb.   Duffel bag of clothes
 7 lb., 4 oz. Shoepacs (two pairs)
 8 lb., 4 oz. Mountain boots (two pairs)
 6 lb., 4 oz. Hip boots (one pair)
 9 lb., 8 oz. Plant presses (two)
 3 lb., 8 oz. First aid kit
20 lb.   Books, papers
65 lb.   10 gal. gasoline (used only 5 gal.)
 5 lb.   miscellaneous

Total weight 332 lbs.

Glossary

algae—A water plant resembling slime.

Arctic—the area north of the Arctic Circle.

bear tree—a tree used by grizzlies as a signpost.

belay—a mountaineering term meaning a system of holding a climber with a rope.

cache—a place to store food, safe from predators, usually high in a tree.

conifer—a cone-bearing tree.

dry tundra—area with good drainage which dries up quickly after a rain.

ermine—short-tailed weasel of the Arctic.

forage—to feed.

frost-heave—places where the earth has opened and frost has forced out wet clay and gravel.

glacier—term used by Alaskans for the non-moving ice sheets which are attached to the ground and are formed when water flows over existing ice in the cold season.

glassing—using binoculars.

grizzly cache—places where grizzlies have covered their meat with soil and vegetation.

Hay Mouse—small rodent, size of a house mouse, which stores food in "hay" piles.

hummocks—solid humps of vegetation, either of moss or of dense grass roots.

overflow ice—(see glacier).

permafrost—ground permanently frozen, usually a foot or so but sometimes only a few inches below the surface.

pingo—large frost-heave.

piton—mountaineering term for steel pins used in the rocks to anchor a climber or belay man.

rappel—mountaineering term for a certain method of sliding down a rope.

rock lichens—plants which grow only a small fraction of an inch thick on rocks.

Sculpins—a small fish, only two or three inches long, which lives in Arctic streams.

Singing Voles—(see Hay Mouse).

sling—mountaineering term for a looped short line, usually used for attaching climber to piton or rope.

territory—the area defended by a bird or other animal for his own use, exclusive of any others of his species.

treeline—the line which defines the northern limit of where spruces (conifers) grow.

tundra—the area north of treeline, where no trees grow.

Tundra Vole—a rodent of the tundra, larger than a Singing Vole.

tussock—firm, thickly matted clumps of cottongrass or other grasses or sedges.

Appendix 1

For Further Reading

Arctic Wilderness. Robert Marshall. Berkeley: University of California Press, 1956.

Wolves of Mount McKinley. Adolph Murie. National Park Service, 1944.

We Live in the Arctic. Constance and Harmon Helmericks. Boston: Little, Brown & Company, 1947.

Arctic Wild. Lois Crisler. New York: Harper, 1956.

Birds of Anaktuvuk Pass, Kobuk and Old Crow. Laurence Irving. Washington, D.C.: Smithsonian Institution, 1960.

Mammals of Northern Alaska. James Bee and Raymond Hall. Lawrence: University of Kansas Museum of Natural History, 1956.

A Naturalist in Alaska. Adolph Murie. New York: Devin-Adair Company, 1961.

Two in the Far North. Margaret Murie. New York: Alfred A. Knopf, 1962.

Birds of the Colville River, Northern Alaska. Brina Kessel and Tom J. Cade. Biological Papers of the University of Alaska, 1958.

Behavior of the Barren-Ground Caribou. William O. Pruitt, Jr. Biological Papers of the University of Alaska, 1960.

Waterfowl Tomorrow. Editor: Joseph P. Linduska. Bureau of Sport Fisheries and Wildlife, Fish and Wildlife Service, United States Department of the Interior, 1964.

"Toxic Substances and Ecological Cycles," by George M. Woodwell. *Scientific American,* March 1967.

Index